Influencer Marketing 2024

A Comprehensive Guide to Building Brands, Strategies, Tips, and Case Studies for Leveraging Social Media Influencers to Grow Your Brand

Heinrich Brevis

Copyright 2024 by Heinrich Brevis - All rights reserved.

This document is geared towards providing exact and reliable information in regards to the topic and issue covered. The publication is sold with the idea that the publisher is not required to render accounting, officially permitted, or otherwise, qualified services. If advice is necessary, legal or professional, a practiced individual in the profession should be ordered.

- From a Declaration of Principles which was accepted and approved equally by a Committee of the American Bar Association and a Committee of Publishers and Associations.

In no way is it legal to reproduce, duplicate, or transmit any part of this document in either electronic means or in printed format. Recording of this publication is strictly prohibited and any storage of this document is not allowed unless with written permission from the publisher. All rights reserved.

The information provided herein is stated to be truthful and consistent, in that any liability, in terms of inattention or otherwise, by any usage or abuse of any policies, processes, or directions contained within is the solitary and utter responsibility of the recipient reader. Under no circumstances will any legal responsibility or blame be held against the publisher for any reparation, damages, or monetary loss due to the information herein, either directly or indirectly.

Respective authors own all copyrights not held by the publisher.

The information herein is offered for informational purposes solely, and is universal as so.

The presentation of the information is without contract or any type of guarantee assurance.

The trademarks that are used are without any consent, and the publication of the trademark is without permission or backing by the trademark owner. All trademarks and brands within this book are for clarifying purposes only and are the owned by the owners themselves, not affiliated with this document

Table of Contents

Introduction 8

Chapter 1: Introduction to Influencer Marketing 12
    1.1 What is Influencer Marketing? 14
    1.2 The Evolution of Influencer Marketing 16
    1.3 The Importance of Influencer Marketing in 2024 20
    1.3 The Importance of Influencer Marketing in 2024 23
    1.5 Challenges and Opportunities in Influencer Marketing 27

Chapter 2: Understanding Social Media Platforms 30
    2.1 Overview of Major Social Media Platforms 33
    2.2 Demographics and User Behavior on Major Social Media Platforms 36
    2.3 Platform-Specific Influencer Marketing Strategies 41
    2.4 Emerging Platforms to Watch in 2024 46

Chapter 3: Identifying the Right Influencers 50
    3.1 Types of Influencers: Mega, Macro, Micro, and Nano 54
    3.2 Tools and Methods for Finding Influencers 59
    3.3 Evaluating Influencer Authenticity and Engagement 63
    3.4 Building Relationships with Influencers 66

Chapter 4: Developing an Influencer Marketing Strategy 70
    4.1 Setting Clear Goals and Objectives 73
    4.2 Budgeting and Resource Allocation 76
    4.3 Crafting a Compelling Brand Message 79
    4.4 Creating a Content Plan and Timeline 82
    4.5 Metrics and KPIs for Measuring Success 86

Chapter 5: Executing Influencer Campaigns 91
Chapter 5: Executing Influencer Campaigns 95
    5.1 Designing Effective Campaigns 98
    5.2 Negotiating Contracts and Agreements 101
    5.3 Best Practices for Collaboration and Communication 105
    5.4 Monitoring and Optimizing Campaign Performance 109

Chapter 6: Legal and Ethical Considerations 114
    6.1 Understanding FTC Guidelines and Regulations 119

6.2 Ensuring Transparency and Authenticity ... 122

6.3 Managing Influencer Relationships and Agreements ... 127

6.4 Ethical Issues in Influencer Marketing ... 132

Chapter 7: Advanced Strategies and Trends ... 138

7.1 Leveraging Data and Analytics ... 144

7.2 Integrating Influencer Marketing with Other Channels ... 150

7.3 The Rise of Virtual Influencers and AI ... 156

7.4 Influencer Marketing in Niche Markets ... 163

7.5 Future Trends to Watch in 2024 and Beyond ... 170

Chapter 8: Measuring ROI and Long-Term Impact ... 179

8.1 Calculating ROI in Influencer Marketing ... 182

8.2 Long-Term Brand Building with Influencers ... 186

8.3 Adjusting Strategies Based on Performance Data ... 188

8.4 Building Sustainable Influencer Partnerships ... 192

Conclusion ... 196

Introduction

In the dynamic world of digital marketing, staying ahead of the curve is paramount. As we navigate through 2024, one strategy continues to dominate the landscape: influencer marketing. What started as a niche tactic has become a cornerstone of brand-building efforts across industries. Welcome to "Influencer Marketing 2024: A Comprehensive Guide to Building Brands, Strategies, Tips, and Case Studies for Leveraging Social Media Influencers to Grow Your Brand."

This guide is designed to be your go-to resource, whether you're a seasoned marketer looking to refine your strategy or a newcomer eager to dive into the world of influencer marketing. With social media platforms evolving rapidly, and consumer behavior shifting in response, the need for updated, practical insights has never been greater.

Why Influencer Marketing?

Influencer marketing leverages the power of social proof. Consumers trust recommendations from individuals they admire and follow, often more than traditional advertisements. By partnering with influencers, brands can reach targeted audiences authentically and engagingly. This approach not only enhances brand awareness but also drives conversions and loyalty.

What You'll Learn

In this book, we'll cover:

- **The Foundations of Influencer Marketing**: Understanding what influencer marketing is, its history, and why it's so effective.
- **Building Your Strategy**: Step-by-step guidance on developing a robust influencer marketing strategy tailored to your brand's goals.
- **Finding the Right Influencers**: Tips on identifying and collaborating with influencers who align with your brand values and audience.
- **Creating Compelling Campaigns**: How to design and execute campaigns that resonate with your target audience and achieve measurable results.
- **Case Studies**: Real-world examples of successful influencer marketing campaigns across various industries, highlighting key takeaways and best practices.
- **Trends and Future Directions**: Insight into emerging trends and predictions for the future of influencer marketing.
- **Legal and Ethical Considerations**: Navigating the complexities of influencer partnerships, including contracts, disclosures, and compliance.

Why This Book?

The influencer marketing landscape is continually shifting, influenced by new platforms, algorithms, and consumer trends. This book compiles the latest research, strategies, and insights to provide a comprehensive, up-to-date guide. We aim to equip you with the knowledge and tools you need to create impactful influencer marketing campaigns that drive real results.

Whether you're a brand looking to enhance your marketing efforts or an individual aspiring to become an influencer, this guide will serve as a valuable resource. Through detailed analysis, practical advice, and inspiring case studies, "Influencer Marketing 2024" will help you navigate the complexities of this dynamic field and harness its full potential.

Let's embark on this journey together and explore the exciting possibilities that influencer marketing holds for 2024 and beyond.

Chapter 1: Introduction to Influencer Marketing

Influencer marketing, a powerful tool in the digital marketing arsenal, has evolved dramatically over the past decade. It leverages individuals with significant social media followings—known as influencers—to promote products, services, or brands. These influencers, who range from celebrities to niche content creators, possess the ability to sway their audience's purchasing decisions through their authentic and relatable content.

At its core, influencer marketing is built on the concept of social proof. Consumers are more likely to trust recommendations from people they admire or perceive as experts in their fields. This trust translates into higher engagement rates and more effective marketing campaigns compared to traditional advertising methods. The rise of social media platforms like Instagram, YouTube, and TikTok has further fueled the growth of influencer marketing, providing a fertile ground for influencers to cultivate their followings and for brands to tap into these engaged audiences.

The origins of influencer marketing can be traced back to celebrity endorsements, where famous personalities would promote products to their fans. However, the digital age has democratized influence, allowing everyday individuals with specialized knowledge or unique perspectives to amass large followings. These micro and macro influencers, despite not having the widespread fame of traditional celebrities, often have highly dedicated and engaged audiences that trust their opinions and recommendations.

The effectiveness of influencer marketing lies in its ability to create authentic connections between brands and consumers. Unlike traditional advertisements, which can sometimes feel impersonal or intrusive, influencer content often blends seamlessly into the influencer's narrative, making it more relatable and less like a sales pitch. This authenticity is crucial, as modern consumers are increasingly skeptical of overt advertising and are more likely to respond positively to genuine, personal recommendations.

In recent years, the scope of influencer marketing has expanded beyond just product promotion. Influencers are now integral to brand storytelling, content creation, and even product development. Brands collaborate with influencers to co-create products, design marketing campaigns, and generate buzz around new launches. This symbiotic relationship benefits both parties: influencers gain credibility and opportunities for monetization, while brands access a ready-made audience and authentic promotional content.

One of the key challenges in influencer marketing is identifying the right influencers to partner with. It's not just about the number of followers an influencer has, but rather the relevance of their audience to the brand's target market and the level of engagement they command. Tools and platforms have emerged to help brands find and evaluate potential influencers, considering factors such as audience demographics, engagement rates, and past performance.

As influencer marketing has grown, so too have the complexities surrounding it. Brands must navigate issues such as ensuring authenticity, managing influencer relationships, and adhering to legal and ethical guidelines. Disclosure of sponsored content, for instance, is a critical aspect that brands and influencers must handle transparently to maintain trust with their audience and comply with regulations.

The future of influencer marketing looks promising, with trends pointing towards even more integrated and innovative collaborations. Emerging technologies, such as artificial intelligence and augmented reality, are set to revolutionize how influencers create content and interact with their followers. Additionally, the increasing emphasis on diversity and inclusion means that brands are seeking out influencers who represent a wider array of backgrounds and perspectives.

In conclusion, influencer marketing has become a vital component of modern marketing strategies. Its ability to foster genuine connections, drive engagement, and deliver measurable results makes it an invaluable tool for brands looking to navigate the digital landscape. As we delve deeper into this guide, we'll explore the strategies, tips, and case studies that will help you harness the power of influencer marketing to grow your brand in 2024 and beyond.

1.1 What is Influencer Marketing?

Influencer marketing is a form of social media marketing that involves endorsements and product placements from influencers—individuals who have a dedicated social following and are viewed as experts within their niche. The power of influencer marketing lies in the trust and authenticity that influencers have built with their audience. Unlike traditional celebrities, influencers often maintain a closer, more interactive relationship with their followers, making their recommendations feel more genuine and persuasive.

The concept of influencer marketing is rooted in the idea of leveraging someone else's influence to achieve marketing goals. Influencers can sway their audience's opinions and behaviors because they have established credibility and trust within a particular community or industry. This trust translates into higher engagement rates and conversion potential, as followers are more likely to act on an influencer's recommendation.

Influencer marketing operates primarily through social media platforms such as Instagram, YouTube, TikTok, and Twitter. These platforms allow influencers to share content that features products or services in a way that feels natural and authentic. For instance, a fitness influencer might post a workout video wearing branded athletic wear, or a beauty vlogger might create a makeup tutorial using a specific brand's products. The key is that the promotion is woven seamlessly into the influencer's regular content, making it more relatable and less intrusive than traditional advertisements.

The influencers themselves can be categorized into different tiers based on their follower count:

- **Mega-influencers**: These are individuals with millions of followers, often celebrities or well-known public figures. They have a broad reach but may not have as deep a connection with their audience as smaller influencers.
- **Macro-influencers**: These influencers typically have between 100,000 to 1 million followers. They have a substantial reach and are often regarded as experts in their fields.
- **Micro-influencers**: With follower counts ranging from 10,000 to 100,000, micro-influencers have a smaller but highly engaged audience. They often have a strong influence within niche markets.
- **Nano-influencers**: These influencers have fewer than 10,000 followers but can be incredibly impactful within very specific communities due to their high engagement rates and close relationships with their audience.

One of the core benefits of influencer marketing is its ability to create authentic content. Influencers produce and share content that aligns with their brand and resonates with their audience, making the promotion feel more genuine. This authenticity is crucial, as modern consumers are increasingly skeptical of traditional advertisements and are more likely to trust recommendations from people they perceive as peers or experts.

Influencer marketing also allows brands to target specific demographics more effectively. By partnering with influencers who have followers that match the brand's target audience, companies can reach potential customers more precisely. This targeted approach can lead to higher conversion rates and a better return on investment compared to broader marketing campaigns.

The rise of influencer marketing has also been fueled by the shift in consumer behavior towards social media. As people spend more time on platforms like Instagram and TikTok, they look to influencers for inspiration, advice, and entertainment. This creates an ideal environment for brands to engage with consumers in a meaningful and impactful way.

In summary, influencer marketing is a strategy that leverages the trust and credibility that influencers have built with their audience to promote products or services. It operates through social media platforms and relies on authentic, relatable content to engage and persuade potential customers. As we continue to explore the various aspects of influencer marketing in this guide, you'll gain a deeper understanding of how to effectively harness this powerful tool to grow your brand.

1.2 The Evolution of Influencer Marketing

The journey of influencer marketing is a fascinating story of how technology, social media, and consumer behavior have converged to create a new paradigm in marketing. To fully appreciate its impact today, it's essential to understand its evolution from traditional celebrity endorsements to the sophisticated digital campaigns we see now.

Early Beginnings: Celebrity Endorsements

The roots of influencer marketing can be traced back to the early days of advertising, where celebrities were used to endorse products. Brands leveraged the fame and popularity of these well-known figures to attract attention and drive sales. Think of Michael Jordan promoting Nike or Marilyn Monroe with Chanel No. 5. These endorsements were effective because they capitalized on the public's admiration for these celebrities, creating a perceived association between the star and the product.

The Rise of Social Media

The landscape began to shift dramatically with the advent of social media in the early 2000s. Platforms like MySpace, Facebook, and later Instagram, YouTube, and Twitter provided individuals with unprecedented access to large audiences. These platforms democratized fame, allowing everyday people to amass followers and influence through the content they created and shared.

As social media grew, so did the number of individuals who could build a following based on their interests and expertise. These new "digital influencers" were different from traditional celebrities; they were often more relatable and accessible to their followers. Their recommendations felt more like advice from a friend rather than a sales pitch, which significantly increased their impact.

The Emergence of Influencer Marketing as a Strategy

By the late 2000s and early 2010s, brands began to recognize the potential of these digital influencers. Early adopters of influencer marketing included beauty brands like MAC and fashion brands like ASOS, which collaborated with YouTube vloggers and Instagram personalities to reach niche audiences. These collaborations often involved product placements, reviews, and giveaways, seamlessly integrated into the influencer's content.

One pivotal moment was the rise of YouTube beauty gurus, who provided tutorials and product reviews to millions of subscribers. Brands quickly realized the value of sending products to these influencers for review, as a positive mention could lead to a significant spike in sales.

The Professionalization of Influencer Marketing

As the effectiveness of influencer marketing became apparent, the industry began to professionalize. Agencies specializing in influencer marketing emerged, offering services such as influencer matchmaking, campaign management, and performance analytics. Platforms like Influencer.co and AspireIQ also developed, helping brands connect with influencers and manage campaigns more efficiently.

During this period, the metrics of success in influencer marketing evolved. Brands began to look beyond follower counts and started to focus on engagement rates, audience demographics, and the authenticity of the influencer's connection with their followers. This shift was driven by the need for more accountable and ROI-focused marketing strategies.

Regulation and Ethical Considerations

With the growth of influencer marketing came increased scrutiny and regulation. In many countries, advertising standards authorities introduced guidelines requiring influencers to disclose sponsored content. This move was aimed at maintaining transparency and trust between influencers and their audiences. For instance, the Federal Trade Commission (FTC) in the United States mandates clear disclosures of any material connections between influencers and brands.

The Current Landscape and Future Trends

Today, influencer marketing is a sophisticated and integral part of digital marketing strategies across various industries. Influencers are not just promoters but also co-creators, collaborating with brands to develop products and campaigns. The diversity of influencers has also expanded, with nano-influencers and micro-influencers playing significant roles due to their highly engaged, niche audiences.

Looking ahead, the future of influencer marketing will likely be shaped by technological advancements and changing consumer preferences. Emerging technologies like artificial intelligence and augmented reality are set to create new possibilities for content creation and audience engagement. Additionally, the push for greater diversity and inclusion is likely to continue, with brands seeking to work with influencers who represent a wide range of backgrounds and perspectives.

In conclusion, the evolution of influencer marketing reflects broader shifts in media consumption, technology, and consumer behavior. From its early days of celebrity endorsements to the current era of digital influencers, this marketing strategy has continually adapted to remain relevant and effective. As we move forward, understanding its history helps us appreciate its current role and anticipate its future developments in the ever-changing digital landscape.

1.3 The Importance of Influencer Marketing in 2024

As we move further into 2024, the landscape of digital marketing continues to evolve, and influencer marketing remains a critical component of successful brand strategies. The importance of influencer marketing today can be attributed to several key factors that underscore its effectiveness and relevance in the current digital ecosystem.

Authenticity and Trust

In an era where consumers are increasingly skeptical of traditional advertising, authenticity is paramount. Influencers offer a unique advantage because they have built genuine relationships with their followers based on trust and authenticity. Their content is perceived as more relatable and trustworthy compared to conventional ads. When influencers endorse a product or service, their followers are more likely to believe in the recommendation, resulting in higher engagement and conversion rates.

Targeted Reach

One of the most significant advantages of influencer marketing is its ability to target specific demographics effectively. Influencers come in various niches, from beauty and fashion to technology and fitness.

Brands can collaborate with influencers whose audience matches their target market, ensuring that their message reaches the right people. This targeted approach minimizes waste and maximizes the return on investment (ROI) by focusing marketing efforts on those most likely to be interested in the product or service.

Enhanced Content Creation

Influencers are often skilled content creators who understand how to engage their audience through compelling visuals, videos, and storytelling. Partnering with influencers allows brands to leverage this creative expertise to produce high-quality content that resonates with their target audience. This collaboration not only enhances the brand's content library but also provides fresh and innovative ways to present products and services.

Social Proof and Credibility

Social proof is a powerful psychological phenomenon where people look to the actions of others to determine their behavior. Influencers provide this social proof by showcasing their use and endorsement of products. When followers see influencers they admire using a product, they are more likely to perceive it as credible and valuable. This endorsement can significantly influence purchasing decisions, especially in industries where trust and recommendations play a crucial role, such as beauty, fashion, and technology.

Engagement and Interaction

Unlike traditional advertisements that are often one-sided, influencer marketing fosters two-way communication. Influencers actively engage with their followers through comments, direct messages, and live sessions, creating a sense of community and interaction. This engagement builds stronger relationships and fosters loyalty among followers. Brands can benefit from this interactive dynamic by participating in conversations, addressing customer queries, and gaining valuable insights into consumer preferences and feedback.

Adaptability and Flexibility

Influencer marketing offers a high degree of adaptability and flexibility, making it suitable for brands of all sizes and industries. Campaigns can be tailored to fit various budgets, from micro-influencer partnerships with smaller budgets to large-scale collaborations with mega-influencers. Additionally, influencer marketing can be adapted to different goals, whether it's increasing brand awareness, driving sales, or launching a new product. This versatility allows brands to experiment and refine their strategies based on performance and feedback.

Measurable Impact

In 2024, the ability to measure the impact of marketing efforts is more critical than ever. Influencer marketing provides various metrics to track and evaluate campaign performance, such as engagement rates, reach, impressions, and conversions. Advanced analytics tools and platforms offer detailed insights into how influencer partnerships contribute to overall marketing goals. This data-driven approach enables brands to make informed decisions, optimize campaigns, and achieve better results.

Staying Competitive

As more brands recognize the value of influencer marketing, it has become a competitive necessity. Brands that do not engage in influencer marketing risk falling behind their competitors who are successfully leveraging this strategy. Staying competitive in 2024 means embracing innovative marketing tactics and continually seeking new ways to connect with consumers. Influencer marketing provides the edge needed to stand out in a crowded digital marketplace.

In summary, the importance of influencer marketing in 2024 is underscored by its ability to deliver authenticity, targeted reach, enhanced content creation, social proof, engagement, adaptability, measurable impact, and competitive advantage. As consumers continue to value genuine connections and personalized experiences, influencer marketing remains a vital tool for brands looking to grow and thrive in the digital age.

1.3 The Importance of Influencer Marketing in 2024

As we move further into 2024, the landscape of digital marketing continues to evolve, and influencer marketing remains a critical component of successful brand strategies. The importance of influencer marketing today can be attributed to several key factors that underscore its effectiveness and relevance in the current digital ecosystem.

Authenticity and Trust

In an era where consumers are increasingly skeptical of traditional advertising, authenticity is paramount. Influencers offer a unique advantage because they have built genuine relationships with their followers based on trust and authenticity. Their content is perceived as more relatable and trustworthy compared to conventional ads. When influencers endorse a product or service, their followers are more likely to believe in the recommendation, resulting in higher engagement and conversion rates.

Targeted Reach

One of the most significant advantages of influencer marketing is its ability to target specific demographics effectively. Influencers come in various niches, from beauty and fashion to technology and fitness. Brands can collaborate with influencers whose audience matches their target market, ensuring that their message reaches the right people. This targeted approach minimizes waste and maximizes the return on investment (ROI) by focusing marketing efforts on those most likely to be interested in the product or service.

Enhanced Content Creation

Influencers are often skilled content creators who understand how to engage their audience through compelling visuals, videos, and storytelling. Partnering with influencers allows brands to leverage this creative expertise to produce high-quality content that resonates with their target audience. This collaboration not only enhances the brand's content library but also provides fresh and innovative ways to present products and services.

Social Proof and Credibility

Social proof is a powerful psychological phenomenon where people look to the actions of others to determine their behavior. Influencers provide this social proof by showcasing their use and endorsement of products. When followers see influencers they admire using a product, they are more likely to perceive it as credible and valuable. This endorsement can significantly influence purchasing decisions, especially in industries where trust and recommendations play a crucial role, such as beauty, fashion, and technology.

Engagement and Interaction

Unlike traditional advertisements that are often one-sided, influencer marketing fosters two-way communication. Influencers actively engage with their followers through comments, direct messages, and live sessions, creating a sense of community and interaction. This engagement builds stronger relationships and fosters loyalty among followers. Brands can benefit from this interactive dynamic by participating in conversations, addressing customer queries, and gaining valuable insights into consumer preferences and feedback.

Adaptability and Flexibility

Influencer marketing offers a high degree of adaptability and flexibility, making it suitable for brands of all sizes and industries. Campaigns can be tailored to fit various budgets, from micro-influencer partnerships with smaller budgets to large-scale collaborations with mega-influencers. Additionally, influencer marketing can be adapted to different goals, whether it's increasing brand awareness, driving sales, or launching a new product. This versatility allows brands to experiment and refine their strategies based on performance and feedback.

Measurable Impact

In 2024, the ability to measure the impact of marketing efforts is more critical than ever. Influencer marketing provides various metrics to track and evaluate campaign performance, such as engagement rates, reach, impressions, and conversions. Advanced analytics tools and platforms offer detailed insights into how influencer partnerships contribute to overall marketing goals. This data-driven approach enables brands to make informed decisions, optimize campaigns, and achieve better results.

Staying Competitive

As more brands recognize the value of influencer marketing, it has become a competitive necessity. Brands that do not engage in influencer marketing risk falling behind their competitors who are successfully leveraging this strategy. Staying competitive in 2024 means embracing innovative marketing tactics and continually seeking new ways to connect with consumers. Influencer marketing provides the edge needed to stand out in a crowded digital marketplace.

In summary, the importance of influencer marketing in 2024 is underscored by its ability to deliver authenticity, targeted reach, enhanced content creation, social proof, engagement, adaptability, measurable impact, and competitive advantage. As consumers continue to value genuine connections and personalized experiences, influencer marketing remains a vital tool for brands looking to grow and thrive in the digital age.

1.5 Challenges and Opportunities in Influencer Marketing

Influencer marketing presents numerous opportunities for brands to connect with audiences authentically and drive engagement. However, it also comes with its own set of challenges that require careful navigation and strategic planning. Let's explore both the challenges and opportunities in influencer marketing:

Challenges

- **Authenticity Concerns**: Maintaining authenticity can be challenging as influencers balance promotional content with maintaining their brand identity. Audiences are quick to detect inauthentic endorsements, which can erode trust and credibility.
- **Finding the Right Influencers**: Identifying influencers who align with the brand's values, target audience, and campaign objectives requires thorough research and vetting. Choosing the wrong

influencer can result in ineffective campaigns and wasted resources.
- **Saturation and Competition**: The increasing popularity of influencer marketing has led to a crowded marketplace, making it challenging for brands to stand out. Competition for influencer partnerships and audience attention continues to intensify.
- **Measurement and ROI**: Measuring the ROI of influencer marketing campaigns can be complex. Determining the impact on brand awareness, engagement, and sales requires reliable metrics and attribution models.
- **Regulatory Compliance**: Adherence to advertising regulations, such as FTC guidelines in the United States, regarding disclosure of sponsored content is crucial. Non-compliance can lead to legal repercussions and damage to brand reputation.

Opportunities

- **Diverse Influencer Ecosystem**: The influencer landscape encompasses a wide range of influencers, from mega-celebrities to micro-influencers with highly engaged niche audiences. This diversity offers brands opportunities to collaborate with influencers who resonate deeply with specific target demographics.
- **Creative Collaboration**: Influencers bring creativity and authenticity to brand campaigns, producing content that captures audience attention and drives engagement. Collaborating with influencers allows brands to leverage their storytelling skills and unique perspectives.
- **Targeted Reach**: Influencer marketing enables precise targeting of niche audiences based on demographics, interests, and behaviors.

Brands can reach potential customers more effectively compared to traditional mass media approaches.
- **Data-Driven Insights**: Advanced analytics tools provide actionable insights into campaign performance, audience engagement, and consumer behavior. Brands can optimize strategies in real time based on data-driven decisions, enhancing overall campaign effectiveness.
- **Long-Term Relationships**: Successful influencer partnerships can evolve into long-term relationships, where influencers become brand advocates. These relationships foster trust, credibility, and loyalty among followers, contributing to sustained brand growth.
- **Innovation and Experimentation**: The evolving nature of influencer marketing encourages innovation and experimentation with new platforms, formats, and technologies. Brands can stay ahead by adapting to emerging trends and consumer preferences.

In conclusion, while influencer marketing offers significant opportunities for brands to engage with audiences and achieve marketing goals, it also presents challenges that require strategic solutions. By understanding and addressing these challenges while leveraging the opportunities, brands can effectively harness the power of influencer marketing to drive meaningful engagement, build brand loyalty, and achieve sustainable business growth in 2024 and beyond.

Chapter 2: Understanding Social Media Platforms

Social media platforms are the bedrock of influencer marketing, providing the stage where influencers and brands connect with their audiences. Each platform offers unique features, demographics, and engagement dynamics that influence how influencer campaigns are executed and perceived. In this chapter, we delve into the major social media platforms shaping influencer marketing strategies today.

The Role of Social Media in Influencer Marketing

Social media platforms serve as the primary channels through which influencers share content, engage with followers, and collaborate with brands. These platforms facilitate direct communication and interaction between influencers and their audiences, fostering authentic relationships and driving engagement.

Platform Overview

1. Instagram

Instagram remains a dominant force in influencer marketing, known for its visual-centric content and storytelling capabilities. Influencers leverage Instagram's features such as posts, stories, IGTV, and reels to showcase products, lifestyles, and experiences. Brands benefit from Instagram's extensive reach and highly engaged user base, making it ideal for visually-driven campaigns and influencer partnerships.

2. YouTube

As a video-sharing platform, YouTube allows influencers to create long-form content, tutorials, reviews, and entertainment that resonate deeply with audiences. YouTube influencers build communities around their channels, offering brands opportunities for product integrations, sponsorships, and collaborations that can drive both brand awareness and direct response.

3. TikTok

TikTok has revolutionized short-form video content, capturing the attention of younger demographics with its engaging, viral-friendly format. Influencers on TikTok excel at creating entertaining and creative content that can quickly gain traction and reach millions of users. Brands leverage TikTok's algorithm-driven discoverability to launch innovative campaigns and engage with a diverse, global audience.

4. Twitter

Known for its real-time updates and concise messaging, Twitter enables influencers to share opinions, trends, and news in a rapid-fire format. Influencers on Twitter often spark conversations, drive trends, and amplify brand messages through retweets, hashtags, and direct interactions with followers. Brands use Twitter to join cultural conversations, showcase thought leadership, and engage in influencer-driven advocacy.

5. Facebook

Facebook remains a robust platform for influencer marketing, particularly for reaching older demographics and niche communities through groups and pages. Influencers on Facebook engage followers through posts, live videos, and community-driven content, fostering deeper connections and driving organic reach. Brands utilize Facebook's advertising tools and influencer collaborations to target specific audiences and achieve diverse marketing objectives.

Choosing the Right Platform

Selecting the appropriate social media platform(s) for influencer marketing depends on various factors, including target audience demographics, campaign goals, content format preferences, and engagement objectives. Each platform offers distinct advantages and challenges that brands must consider when planning influencer strategies.

Trends and Innovations

Social media platforms continue to evolve, introducing new features, algorithms, and user behaviors that shape influencer marketing strategies. Emerging trends such as live streaming, AR filters, shoppable posts, and platform integrations offer brands and influencers opportunities to innovate and engage audiences in more interactive and immersive ways.

Understanding the role of social media platforms in influencer marketing is crucial for developing effective and impactful campaigns. By leveraging the unique strengths of each platform and staying abreast of evolving trends, brands can maximize their reach, engagement, and ROI through strategic influencer partnerships. In the following chapters, we explore how to harness these platforms to create compelling influencer marketing campaigns that resonate with target audiences and drive business growth.

2.1 Overview of Major Social Media Platforms

Social media platforms play a pivotal role in influencer marketing, offering diverse opportunities for brands to connect with audiences through authentic and engaging content. Understanding the characteristics, demographics, and engagement dynamics of major social media platforms is essential for crafting effective influencer marketing strategies. Here's an overview of the key platforms shaping influencer marketing today:

1. **Instagram**

- **Overview**: Instagram is a visual-centric platform known for its emphasis on photos and videos. It features various content formats, including posts, stories, IGTV, and reels, allowing influencers to showcase products, lifestyles, and experiences creatively.
- **Audience**: Predominantly younger demographics, with a strong presence among Millennials and Gen Z. Popular among fashion, beauty, travel, and lifestyle influencers.

- **Engagement**: High engagement rates due to visually appealing content and interactive features like polls, Q&A, and swipe-up links in stories. Influencers build communities and foster deeper connections with followers through authentic storytelling.

2. YouTube

- **Overview**: YouTube is the largest video-sharing platform globally, offering long-form content such as tutorials, reviews, vlogs, and entertainment. Influencers on YouTube create communities around their channels and engage viewers through subscriber interactions and comments.
- **Audience**: Diverse demographics with a broad age range. Popular among tech enthusiasts, gamers, beauty gurus, and educational content creators.
- **Engagement**: High engagement levels with longer watch times and subscriber loyalty. Influencers integrate products seamlessly into video content, providing in-depth reviews and demonstrations that influence purchasing decisions.

3. TikTok

- **Overview**: TikTok is a short-form video platform known for its viral content and algorithm-driven discoverability. Influencers on TikTok create entertaining and engaging videos, often leveraging trends and challenges to reach a global audience quickly.
- **Audience**: Predominantly younger demographics, including Gen Z and younger Millennials. Popular categories include comedy, dance, fashion, and DIY.

- **Engagement**: High engagement rates with content going viral based on likes, shares, and comments. Brands utilize TikTok's creative tools and trends to launch innovative campaigns and engage with a diverse audience.

4. Twitter

- **Overview**: Twitter is a real-time microblogging platform where influencers share updates, opinions, and news. It's known for its concise messaging, trending topics, and direct interactions through tweets and hashtags.
- **Audience**: Diverse demographics with a strong presence among professionals, journalists, and thought leaders. Popular topics include news, politics, technology, and entertainment.
- **Engagement**: Influencers drive conversations, amplify brand messages, and participate in trending topics through retweets and replies. Brands use Twitter for real-time marketing, customer service, and influencer-driven advocacy.

5. Facebook

- **Overview**: Facebook is a comprehensive social networking platform with diverse content formats, including posts, live videos, and groups. It facilitates community building and personalized interactions among users.
- **Audience**: Wide-ranging demographics, with a significant presence among older adults and families. Popular categories include lifestyle, parenting, health, and local businesses.

- **Engagement**: Influencers engage followers through organic posts, live streams, and community-driven content. Brands utilize Facebook's advertising tools and influencer collaborations to target specific audiences and achieve marketing goals.

Choosing the Right Platform

Selecting the appropriate social media platform(s) for influencer marketing depends on several factors, including target audience demographics, campaign goals, content format preferences, and engagement objectives. Each platform offers unique strengths and challenges that brands must consider when planning influencer strategies.

Understanding the characteristics and audience dynamics of major social media platforms is essential for developing successful influencer marketing campaigns. By leveraging the unique features and engagement opportunities of each platform, brands can maximize their reach, drive meaningful interactions, and achieve their marketing objectives effectively in today's competitive digital landscape.

2.2 Demographics and User Behavior on Major Social Media Platforms

Understanding the demographics and user behavior on major social media platforms is crucial for crafting targeted and effective influencer marketing campaigns. Here's an overview of the demographics and behavior patterns on key platforms influencing influencer marketing strategies today:

1. **Instagram**

Demographics:

- **Age**: Predominantly younger demographics, with a significant user base among Millennials and Gen Z.
- **Gender**: Slightly more female users than male.
- **Location**: Global reach, with high usage in urban areas and developed countries.
- **Interests**: Fashion, beauty, travel, lifestyle, fitness, and food are popular categories.

User Behavior:

- **Engagement**: High engagement rates due to visually appealing content and interactive features like stories, polls, and Q&A.
- **Content Consumption**: Users actively discover new trends, products, and lifestyles through influencer content.
- **Influence**: Influencers build communities and trust through authentic storytelling and personal connections with followers.

2. **YouTube**

Demographics:

- **Age**: Diverse age range, with a significant presence among Millennials and Gen Z, as well as older demographics.
- **Gender**: Balanced user base with slightly more male users in some categories like gaming and tech.
- **Location**: Global reach with localized content based on language and cultural preferences.
- **Interests**: Tech reviews, gaming, beauty tutorials, educational content, and entertainment are popular.

User Behavior:

- **Engagement**: Longer watch times and loyal subscriber bases contribute to high engagement levels.
- **Content Consumption**: Users seek in-depth information, tutorials, reviews, and entertainment across various niches.
- **Influence**: Influencers provide detailed product demonstrations and reviews that impact purchasing decisions.

3. **TikTok**

Demographics:

- **Age**: Predominantly younger demographics, including Gen Z and younger Millennials.
- **Gender**: Balanced user base with slightly more female users in some categories.
- **Location**: Global reach with localized content based on regional trends and challenges.

- **Interests**: Dance challenges, comedy skits, DIY projects, fashion trends, and viral content dominate.

User Behavior:

- **Engagement**: High engagement rates are driven by viral content, likes, shares, and comments.
- **Content Consumption**: Users participate in trends and challenges, and discover new content through personalized feeds.
- **Influence**: Trendsetting behaviors and viral content quickly influence global audiences and consumer behaviors.

4. Twitter

Demographics:

- **Age**: Diverse age range, with a strong presence among professionals, journalists, and younger demographics.
- **Gender**: Balanced user base with a slightly more male-dominated presence in some categories.
- **Location**: Global reach with high usage in urban areas and among tech-savvy users.
- **Interests**: News updates, politics, technology trends, entertainment, and cultural discussions are popular.

User Behavior:

- **Engagement**: Real-time interactions through tweets, retweets, hashtags, and direct conversations.
- **Content Consumption**: Users engage in discussions, share news updates, and amplify trending topics.
- **Influence**: Influencers drive conversations, amplify brand messages, and influence public opinion through thought leadership and advocacy.

5. Facebook

Demographics:

- **Age**: Wide-ranging demographics, with a significant presence among older adults and families.
- **Gender**: Balanced user base with a slightly more female-dominated presence in some categories.
- **Location**: Global reach with localized content based on community and interest groups.
- **Interests**: Lifestyle updates, parenting tips, health information, local businesses, and community-driven content.

User Behavior:

- **Engagement**: Users participate in community groups, share personal updates, and engage with live videos and local events.
- **Content Consumption**: Users discover content through personalized feeds, group interactions, and family connections.

- **Influence**: Influencers build trust through organic posts, live interactions, and community-driven advocacy.

Strategic Considerations

When planning influencer marketing campaigns, brands should consider:

- **Target Audience**: Choose platforms that align with the demographics and interests of the target audience.
- **Content Format**: Tailor content formats (e.g., images, videos, stories) to suit platform-specific engagement behaviors.
- **Engagement Strategies**: Leverage platform features (e.g., hashtags, trends, live videos) to maximize engagement and reach.
- **Campaign Goals**: Align influencer collaborations with specific marketing objectives (e.g., brand awareness, product launch, and sales promotion).

By understanding the unique demographics and user behaviors across major social media platforms, brands can effectively leverage influencer partnerships to engage audiences authentically, drive conversions, and achieve sustainable growth in today's competitive digital landscape.

2.3 Platform-Specific Influencer Marketing Strategies

Influencer marketing strategies must be tailored to each social media platform's unique features, audience demographics, and engagement dynamics to maximize effectiveness. Here's a platform-specific guide to crafting successful influencer marketing strategies:

1. Instagram

Strategy Highlights:

- **Visual Storytelling**: Leverage high-quality images and videos to showcase products or services in authentic, lifestyle-oriented settings.
- **Instagram Stories**: Use ephemeral content to provide behind-the-scenes glimpses, product tutorials, and interactive polls to engage followers.
- **Influencer Takeovers**: Allow influencers to temporarily control brand accounts to create authentic, real-time content and increase reach.
- **Hashtag Campaigns**: Create branded hashtags to encourage user-generated content (UGC) and amplify campaign visibility.

2. YouTube

Strategy Highlights:

- **Long-Form Content**: Collaborate with influencers to create detailed product reviews, tutorials, and educational content that align with audience interests.

- **Product Integrations**: Integrate products seamlessly into influencer videos to demonstrate features, benefits, and usage scenarios.
- **Collaborative Videos**: Partner with influencers on co-created content, interviews, or challenge videos to leverage their expertise and engage subscribers.
- **Endorsement Videos**: Sponsor influencer-created content that aligns with brand values and resonates with the target audience.

3. TikTok

Strategy Highlights:

- **Short-Form Viral Content**: Create engaging, entertaining videos that align with TikTok trends, challenges, and viral content formats.
- **Influencer Challenges**: Launch branded challenges and collaborate with influencers to encourage user participation and content creation.
- **Authenticity and Creativity**: Emphasize authenticity and creativity in influencer content to resonate with TikTok's youthful and trend-focused audience.
- **Trendjacking**: Participate in trending topics and hashtags to increase brand visibility and relevance within the TikTok community.

4. Twitter

Strategy Highlights:

- **Real-Time Engagement**: Engage in real-time conversations, reply to tweets, and participate in trending topics to increase brand visibility and foster community interaction.
- **Thought Leadership**: Position influencers as thought leaders by sharing insights, industry updates, and valuable content that resonates with Twitter's professional and tech-savvy audience.
- **Twitter Chats**: Host or participate in Twitter chats with influencers to discuss relevant topics, share expertise, and engage with followers in meaningful conversations.
- **Campaign Amplification**: Amplify influencer-created content through retweets, hashtags, and sponsored tweets to reach a wider audience and increase campaign impact.

5. Facebook

Strategy Highlights:

- **Community Engagement**: Engage with local communities, interest groups, and niche audiences through influencer collaborations and organic posts.
- **Live Video Events**: Host live video events with influencers to showcase products, conduct Q&A sessions, and interact with followers in real time.

- **Group Interactions**: Participate in Facebook groups relevant to the brand's niche to build credibility, and trust, and foster deeper connections with community members.
- **Storytelling and Testimonials**: Share influencer-generated stories and testimonials that highlight product benefits and customer experiences to resonate with Facebook's diverse audience.

Key Considerations

- **Platform Alignment**: Select platforms based on audience demographics, content preferences, and engagement behaviors that align with campaign objectives.
- **Content Strategy**: Tailor content formats, messaging, and storytelling techniques to suit each platform's unique features and audience expectations.
- **Influencer Selection**: Choose influencers whose content style, values, and audience demographics align with the brand's target market and campaign goals.
- **Measurement and Optimization**: Utilize platform analytics and performance metrics to track campaign success, optimize strategies in real time, and maximize ROI.

By implementing platform-specific influencer marketing strategies, brands can effectively leverage the strengths of each social media platform to engage audiences authentically, drive brand awareness, and foster meaningful connections that resonate in today's dynamic digital landscape.

2.4 Emerging Platforms to Watch in 2024

In 2024, several emerging social media platforms are gaining traction and presenting new opportunities for influencer marketing. These platforms offer unique features, demographics, and engagement dynamics that brands can leverage to reach and engage with their target audiences effectively. Here are some emerging platforms to watch in 2024:

1. Clubhouse

- **Overview**: Clubhouse is an audio-based social networking platform that allows users to join virtual rooms for live discussions, panels, and networking sessions. It focuses on real-time, voice-only interactions.
- **Audience**: Primarily professionals, entrepreneurs, and thought leaders interested in industry insights, networking opportunities, and knowledge-sharing.
- **Influencer Opportunities**: Influencers can host rooms to discuss industry trends, host Q&A sessions, and share expertise. Brands can collaborate with influencers to sponsor rooms, participate in discussions, and reach a highly engaged audience.

2. Discord

- **Overview**: Discord is a communication platform initially designed for gamers but has expanded to include various interest groups and

communities. It features text, voice, and video chat capabilities within customizable servers.
- **Audience**: Diverse audience segments, including gamers, tech enthusiasts, artists, and niche interest groups.
- **Influencer Opportunities**: Influencers create communities (servers) around specific topics or interests, fostering engagement through discussions, events, and exclusive content. Brands can partner with influencers to sponsor server events, host AMA sessions, and engage with community members authentically.

3. **Snapchat**

- **Overview**: Snapchat is a multimedia messaging app known for its disappearing photo and video messages (snaps) and augmented reality (AR) filters. It also features Stories and Discover content.
- **Audience**: Predominantly younger demographics, including Gen Z and Millennials, are interested in creative content, AR experiences, and ephemeral messaging.
- **Influencer Opportunities**: Influencers on Snapchat create engaging Stories, use AR lenses to promote products, and collaborate with brands for sponsored content. Brands can leverage Snapchat's engaging features to launch interactive campaigns and reach a youthful, tech-savvy audience.

4. **Twitch**

- **Overview**: Twitch is a live streaming platform primarily focused on gaming content, including gameplay streams, esports tournaments, and creative arts broadcasts.

- **Audience**: Gaming enthusiasts, esports fans, and creative content creators, spanning diverse demographics with a strong male presence.
- **Influencer Opportunities**: Influencers (streamers) build loyal fan bases through live streaming, interactive chats, and subscriptions. Brands can sponsor streams, collaborate on branded content, and reach engaged audiences interested in gaming, tech, and entertainment.

5. Pinterest

- **Overview**: Pinterest is a visual discovery and bookmarking platform where users discover and save ideas through images and videos (pins). It features boards for organizing and curating content.
- **Audience**: Mainly female users interested in fashion, home decor, DIY projects, recipes, and lifestyle inspiration.
- **Influencer Opportunities**: Influencers on Pinterest curate inspirational boards, create tutorials, and showcase products through visually appealing pins. Brands can collaborate on sponsored pins, promoted content, and influencer-curated boards to drive traffic, brand awareness, and purchase intent.

Strategic Considerations

- **Audience Alignment**: Choose platforms based on audience demographics, interests, and engagement behaviors that align with campaign goals.

- **Content Strategy**: Tailor content formats (e.g., audio, video, images) and messaging to suit each platform's unique features and user preferences.
- **Influencer Selection**: Partner with influencers whose content resonates with the platform's audience and complements the brand's values and objectives.
- **Measurement and Optimization**: Utilize platform analytics to track performance, optimize campaigns, and maximize ROI through data-driven insights.

By exploring emerging platforms like Clubhouse, Discord, Snapchat, Twitch, and Pinterest in 2024, brands can innovate their influencer marketing strategies, engage with niche audiences, and stay ahead in the competitive digital landscape.

Chapter 3: Identifying the Right Influencers

Choosing the right influencers is crucial for the success of influencer marketing campaigns. This chapter explores effective strategies and criteria for identifying influencers who align with your brand's values, target audience, and campaign objectives.

Understanding Influencer Types

1. Mega-Influencers

- **Reach**: Millions of followers across multiple platforms.
- **Audience**: Wide reach but less niche-specific.
- **Use Case**: Ideal for broad brand awareness campaigns and large-scale promotions.

2. Macro-Influencers

- **Reach**: Hundreds of thousands to millions of followers.
- **Audience**: Niche-specific with a significant following.
- **Use Case**: Effective for targeted campaigns reaching specific demographics or interests.

3. Micro-Influencers

- **Reach**: Few thousand to under a hundred thousand followers.

- **Audience**: Highly engaged and niche-focused.
- **Use Case**: Best for authentic engagement, niche markets, and localized campaigns.

4. Nano-Influencers

- **Reach**: Typically less than ten thousand followers.
- **Audience**: Hyper-local and deeply engaged.
- **Use Case**: Extremely targeted campaigns, high authenticity, and community-focused promotions.

Criteria for Selecting Influencers

1. Relevance

- Ensure the influencer's content aligns with your brand's values, industry, and target audience demographics.
- Analyze their content themes, style, and audience engagement to gauge relevance.

2. Engagement

- Look beyond follower count to evaluate engagement metrics such as likes, comments, shares, and overall interaction rates.
- High engagement indicates an influencer's ability to connect authentically with their audience.

3. Authenticity

- Assess the influencer's authenticity based on their content quality, voice, and transparency in sponsored posts.
- Authentic influencers maintain credibility and trust, enhancing the effectiveness of brand collaborations.

4. Reach and Influence

- Consider the influencer's reach in terms of audience size and demographic relevance.
- Evaluate their influence in driving actions such as website visits, product purchases, or social media shares.

5. Consistency and Reputation

- Review the influencer's posting frequency, content consistency, and reputation within their community.
- Consistent influencers build trust and long-term relationships with their audience and brands.

Tools and Strategies for Identification

1. Influencer Platforms

- Utilize influencer marketing platforms (e.g., Upfluence, AspireIQ) to discover and connect with influencers based on specific criteria and metrics.
- These platforms offer insights into influencer performance, audience demographics, and campaign history.

2. Social Listening and Monitoring

- Monitor social media platforms and industry trends to identify emerging influencers and viral content.
- Use hashtags, mentions, and search queries to find relevant influencers discussing topics related to your brand.

3. Relationship Building

- Build relationships with influencers through direct outreach, collaborations, and personalized engagement.
- Cultivate partnerships based on mutual interests, shared values, and aligned goals for long-term collaborations.

4. Data Analytics

- Leverage analytics tools to track influencer performance, campaign ROI, and audience insights.
- Measure key metrics such as engagement rates, click-through rates, and conversion rates to optimize influencer partnerships.

Identifying the right influencers involves a strategic approach that considers relevance, engagement, authenticity, reach, consistency, and reputation. By selecting influencers who resonate with your brand's values and connect authentically with your target audience, you can create impactful influencer marketing campaigns that drive brand awareness, engagement, and conversions effectively. In the following chapters, we explore strategies for engaging influencers, negotiating partnerships, and measuring campaign success to maximize ROI and achieve long-term business growth.

3.1 Types of Influencers: Mega, Macro, Micro, and Nano

Influencers play a pivotal role in shaping brand perceptions and driving consumer behavior in the digital age. Understanding the different types of influencers based on their reach and audience engagement is crucial for developing effective influencer marketing strategies. Here's an overview of the main types of influencers:

1. **Mega-Influencers**

Reach:

Typically have millions of followers across various social media platforms.

Audience:

Broad and diverse, often spanning across different demographics and regions.

Use Case:

Ideal for large-scale brand awareness campaigns and for reaching a massive audience quickly.

Example:

Celebrities, industry leaders, and top-tier social media personalities.

2. Macro-Influencers

Reach:

Have hundreds of thousands to millions of followers.

Audience:

Niche-specific with a substantial following interested in specific topics or industries.

Use Case:

Effective for targeted campaigns aimed at specific demographics or interest groups.

Example:

Industry experts, popular bloggers, and content creators with a significant following.

3. Micro-Influencers

Reach:

Typically have a few thousand to under a hundred thousand followers.

Audience:

Highly engaged and niche-focused, often sharing specific interests or lifestyles.

Use Case:

Best for fostering authentic engagement, niche markets, and localized campaigns.

Example:

Specialized bloggers, local celebrities, and community influencers.

4. Nano-Influencers

Reach:

Generally have less than ten thousand followers.

Audience:

Hyper-localized and deeply engaged, often within a specific community or neighborhood.

Use Case:

Suitable for highly targeted campaigns, grassroots marketing efforts, and community-driven promotions.

Example:

Local activists, enthusiasts, and micro-bloggers with a dedicated local following.

Choosing the Right Influencer Type

- **Campaign Objectives**: Align influencer type with campaign goals, whether it's to increase brand awareness, drive engagement, or boost sales.
- **Target Audience**: Consider which influencer type best resonates with your target audience's demographics, interests, and behaviors.
- **Budget and Resources**: Evaluate the scalability and cost-effectiveness of each influencer type based on your budget and resources.

Strategic Considerations

- **Mixing Influencer Types**: Consider combining different influencer types to leverage their strengths and maximize campaign impact.
- **Engagement vs. Reach**: Balance between influencer reach and audience engagement metrics to achieve campaign objectives effectively.
- **Long-term Relationships**: Cultivate long-term partnerships with influencers aligned with your brand values and audience preferences for sustained marketing success.

Understanding the nuances between mega, macro, micro, and nano influencers empowers brands to leverage influencer marketing effectively, build meaningful connections with target audiences, and achieve measurable business outcomes in today's competitive digital landscape.

3.2 Tools and Methods for Finding Influencers

Identifying the right influencers for your brand involves using effective tools and methods to ensure alignment with your campaign goals, target audience, and brand values. Here are some tools and strategies to find influencers:

1. Influencer Marketing Platforms

Tools:

- **Upfluence**: Offers influencer search based on audience demographics, engagement metrics, and content relevance.
- **AspireIQ**: Provides influencer discovery, relationship management, and campaign tracking features.
- **Influence.co**: Allows brands to search for influencers by niche, location, and social media platform.

Method:

- Use these platforms to filter influencers based on criteria such as follower demographics, engagement rates, past collaborations, and performance metrics.

2. Social Media Listening and Monitoring

Tools:

- **Brandwatch**: Monitors social media platforms for brand mentions, industry trends, and influencer discussions.
- **Hootsuite**: Tracks hashtags, mentions, and keywords across social networks to identify influential voices in your industry.

Method:

- Monitor conversations, hashtags, and trending topics related to your brand or industry to discover relevant influencers organically.

3. Google and Social Media Searches

Tools:

- **Google Search**: Use specific keywords (e.g., "top fashion influencers 2024") to find influencer lists, articles, and blogs featuring industry leaders.
- **Social Media Platforms**: Use platform-specific search tools to discover influencers by name, hashtags, or topics of interest.

Method:

- Conduct searches on Google and social media platforms to identify influencers based on their content, engagement levels, and audience demographics.

4. Content Creators and Bloggers

Tools:

- **BuzzSumo**: Identifies top-performing content and influential bloggers by topic, allowing brands to connect with relevant creators.
- **NinjaOutreach**: Facilitates outreach to bloggers and content creators for collaborations and influencer partnerships.

Method:

- Explore blogs, websites, and content platforms within your industry to find influential bloggers and content creators who align with your brand values.

5. Agency and Network Partnerships

Tools:

- **Influencer Agencies**: Partner with agencies specializing in influencer marketing to access curated influencer networks and campaign management services.
- **Network Platforms**: Join influencer networks and communities (e.g., Tribe, TapInfluence) to connect with verified influencers across different categories.

Method:

- Collaborate with influencer agencies or network platforms to leverage their expertise in identifying, negotiating with, and managing influencer partnerships.

Best Practices

- **Define Criteria**: Clearly define influencer criteria based on campaign goals, audience demographics, content relevance, and engagement metrics.
- **Engagement Assessment**: Evaluate influencers based on engagement rates, authenticity, and alignment with brand values rather than follower count alone.
- **Relationship Building**: Establish genuine relationships with influencers through personalized outreach, mutual respect, and transparent communication.
- **Performance Tracking**: Use analytics tools to track influencer performance, measure campaign ROI, and optimize strategies based on real-time data insights.

By leveraging these tools and methods for finding influencers, brands can effectively identify and collaborate with the right influencers to drive brand awareness, engagement, and conversions in influencer marketing campaigns.

3.3 Evaluating Influencer Authenticity and Engagement

Authenticity and engagement are crucial factors when evaluating influencers for collaboration in influencer marketing campaigns. Here's how to effectively assess these aspects:

1. **Authenticity Assessment**

Indicators of Authenticity:

- **Content Quality**: Evaluate the influencer's content for consistency, creativity, and relevance to their niche.
- **Voice and Tone**: Assess how genuine and aligned the influencer's voice is with their audience and brand values.
- **Transparency**: Look for clear disclosures of sponsored content and genuine recommendations.

Methods:

- **Content Review**: Analyze the influencer's past posts, captions, and interactions to gauge authenticity.

- **Audience Interaction**: Review comments, likes, and shares to assess the level of engagement and trust among followers.
- **Sponsored Content**: Evaluate how influencers integrate sponsored content seamlessly into their feed without compromising authenticity.

2. Engagement Evaluation

Key Engagement Metrics:

- **Likes and Comments**: Measure the average number of likes and comments per post to gauge audience interaction.
- **Shares and Saves**: Assess how frequently followers share and save the influencer's content, indicating deeper engagement.
- **Response Rate**: Evaluate how often the influencer responds to comments and interacts with their audience.

Methods:

- **Engagement Rate Calculation**: Calculate the engagement rate (likes + comments + shares) per post divided by the total number of followers to normalize against follower count.
- **Audience Sentiment**: Monitor sentiment analysis of comments and interactions to understand audience perception and engagement levels.
- **Comparative Analysis**: Compare engagement metrics across similar influencers or competitor campaigns to benchmark performance.

3. Tools for Evaluation

Tools:

- **Social Media Analytics**: Platforms like Instagram Insights, YouTube Analytics, and Twitter Analytics provide data on engagement metrics, audience demographics, and content performance.
- **Influencer Marketing Platforms**: Tools such as Upfluence, AspireIQ, and Hootsuite offer influencer analytics for evaluating authenticity, engagement rates, and performance metrics.
- **Third-Party Tools**: Use sentiment analysis tools, like Brandwatch or Sprout Social, to assess audience sentiment and influencer credibility.

Usage:

- **Data-driven Insights**: Utilize analytics tools to gather quantitative data and insights on influencer performance, audience demographics, and engagement trends.
- **Qualitative Assessment**: Combine quantitative data with qualitative assessments of content quality, brand alignment, and audience interaction to make informed decisions.

4. Considerations for Authentic Engagement

- **Long-term Impact**: Prioritize influencers who foster genuine connections with their audience, leading to sustained brand loyalty and advocacy.
- **Brand Fit**: Ensure influencers align with your brand values and messaging to maintain authenticity in content collaborations.
- **Transparency**: Collaborate with influencers who are transparent about partnerships and maintain trust with their audience through honest recommendations.

By effectively evaluating influencer authenticity and engagement, brands can identify trustworthy partners who resonate with their target audience, drive meaningful interactions, and maximize the impact of influencer marketing campaigns.

3.4 Building Relationships with Influencers

Building strong relationships with influencers is essential for successful influencer marketing campaigns. Here's a comprehensive guide on how to cultivate and maintain meaningful partnerships with influencers:

1. **Research and Personalization**

   - **Understand Influencers**: Research potential influencers thoroughly to grasp their content style, audience demographics, values, and engagement metrics.
   - **Personalized Outreach**: Craft personalized messages that highlight why you admire their work and how collaboration can be mutually beneficial.

2. **Transparent Communication**

   - **Honesty and Clarity**: Communicate campaign objectives, expectations, deliverables, and compensation terms upfront.
   - **Feedback Loop**: Maintain open communication channels for feedback, questions, and concerns throughout the collaboration.

3. **Offer Value and Benefits**

   - **Mutual Benefits**: Highlight how the collaboration can benefit the influencer, such as exposure to a new audience, exclusive access, or professional opportunities.
   - **Compensation**: Fairly compensate influencers for their time, creativity, and audience reach, considering their influence and market rates.

4. **Engagement and Support**

   - **Active Engagement**: Engage with influencers' content regularly by liking, commenting, and sharing to show genuine interest and support.
   - **Promotion**: Promote influencers' content on your brand's channels to reciprocate and amplify their reach.

5. **Collaborative Content Creation**

- **Creative Freedom**: Provide influencers with creative freedom to align branded content with their authentic voice and audience preferences.
- **Co-Creation**: Collaborate on content ideas, campaigns, and strategies to leverage influencers' expertise and creativity.

6. **Long-Term Partnerships**

- **Relationship Building**: Invest in long-term relationships by nurturing trust, reliability, and mutual respect beyond individual campaigns.
- **Exclusive Opportunities**: Offer exclusive opportunities, such as product launches, events, or ambassadorships, to deepen partnerships.

7. **Measure and Optimize Performance**

- **Performance Metrics**: Use analytics tools to track campaign performance, including engagement rates, conversions, and ROI.
- **Optimization**: Analyze data insights to optimize future campaigns, refine strategies, and maximize influencer partnerships' effectiveness.

8. **Legal and Ethical Considerations**

- **Compliance**: Ensure influencers disclose sponsored content transparently and comply with advertising guidelines and regulations.

- **Contracts**: Use contracts outlining terms, deliverables, exclusivity, and rights to protect both parties and clarify expectations.

9. **Recognition and Appreciation**

- **Acknowledgment**: Acknowledge and celebrate influencers' contributions publicly and privately to foster loyalty and motivation.
- **Feedback**: Provide constructive feedback and recognition for successful collaborations to strengthen relationships.

10. **Adaptability and Flexibility**

- **Adapt to Changes**: Be flexible and adaptable to influencers' evolving needs, market trends, and audience preferences.
- **Feedback Integration**: Integrate influencers' feedback and suggestions into future campaigns to enhance collaboration and outcomes.

Building relationships with influencers requires dedication, transparency, and a genuine interest in mutual success. By fostering trust, offering value, and maintaining open communication, brands can cultivate lasting partnerships that drive impactful influencer marketing campaigns and achieve long-term business growth.

Chapter 4: Developing an Influencer Marketing Strategy

In today's digital landscape, influencer marketing has evolved into a cornerstone strategy for brands aiming to amplify their reach, engage with audiences authentically, and drive conversions. Developing a comprehensive influencer marketing strategy involves strategic planning, thoughtful execution, and continuous optimization to maximize impact and achieve business objectives effectively.

1. **Define Your Objectives**

Before diving into influencer collaborations, it's crucial to define clear and measurable objectives. Whether your goal is to increase brand awareness, boost engagement, drive sales, or launch new products/services, setting specific objectives provides direction and benchmarks for success. Each objective should be aligned with broader marketing goals and tailored to fit the unique strengths of influencer partnerships.

2. **Identify Your Target Audience**

Understanding your target audience is fundamental to selecting the right influencers and crafting resonant messaging. Define demographics, interests, behaviors, and preferences to pinpoint where your audience engages most—whether it's on Instagram, YouTube, TikTok, or other platforms. This knowledge guides influencer selection, ensuring their followers align closely with your ideal customer profile.

3. **Select the Right Influencers**

Choosing influencers who resonate authentically with your brand and audience is paramount. Consider factors beyond follower counts, such as engagement rates, content quality, and alignment with your brand values. Mega, macro, micro, or nano influencers each offer unique benefits depending on campaign goals—whether it's broad reach, niche expertise, or hyper-localized influence.

4. **Set a Budget and Allocate Resources**

Effective influencer marketing requires a well-defined budget that covers influencer fees, content creation costs, campaign management, and analytics tools. Allocate resources strategically to maximize ROI while ensuring influencers are compensated fairly for their creative contributions and audience access.

5. **Develop Content and Campaign Strategies**

Collaborate closely with influencers to develop compelling content that resonates authentically with their audience while aligning with your brand's messaging and campaign goals. Establish clear guidelines, creative briefs, and content calendars to maintain consistency across platforms and ensure seamless integration of brand messaging within influencer-generated content.

6. Execute and Manage Campaigns

Launch campaigns with a focus on maintaining brand integrity and compliance with legal guidelines. Monitor influencer posts, engage with audience interactions, and respond promptly to feedback or inquiries. Use analytics tools to track performance metrics such as engagement rates, click-through rates, and conversions in real time, enabling agile adjustments to optimize campaign effectiveness.

7. Measure ROI and Evaluate Success

Evaluate campaign success based on predefined KPIs, including quantitative metrics (e.g., ROI, sales lift) and qualitative insights (e.g., audience sentiment, brand perception). Analyze data to identify successful strategies, areas for improvement, and opportunities for future optimizations. This iterative process ensures continuous learning and refinement of influencer marketing strategies.

8. Build Long-Term Relationships

Nurture relationships with influencers beyond individual campaigns by fostering mutual respect, transparency, and shared goals. Offer ongoing opportunities for collaboration, such as ambassador programs or exclusive partnerships, to sustain engagement and leverage influencer advocacy over time.

9. **Legal and Compliance Considerations**

Ensure compliance with regulatory requirements and industry guidelines, such as FTC disclosures for sponsored content. Use contracts or agreements to formalize partnerships, clarify deliverables, and protect both parties' rights, mitigating potential risks associated with influencer collaborations.

10. **Adapt and Innovate**

Stay agile and responsive to evolving market trends, platform updates, and consumer behaviors. Incorporate influencer feedback, audience insights, and competitive analysis into future strategies to innovate and stay ahead in the competitive influencer marketing landscape.

A well-crafted influencer marketing strategy integrates strategic planning, data-driven insights, creative collaboration, and meticulous execution to achieve tangible business outcomes. By defining clear objectives, selecting the right influencers, crafting compelling content, and measuring performance rigorously, brands can harness the power of influencer partnerships to build brand credibility, expand audience reach, and foster meaningful connections in the digital age.

4.1 Setting Clear Goals and Objectives

Setting clear goals and objectives is foundational to a successful influencer marketing strategy. These goals provide direction, focus efforts, and serve as benchmarks for measuring campaign success.

Here's how to establish effective goals and objectives for your influencer marketing initiatives:

1. Define Specific Goals

- **Brand Awareness**: Increase visibility and recognition of your brand among target audiences.
- **Audience Engagement**: Foster meaningful interactions and dialogue with your audience.
- **Lead Generation**: Drive traffic, leads, and conversions to your website or landing pages.
- **Product Launches**: Successfully introduce new products or services to the market.
- **Content Amplification**: Extend the reach and impact of your content through influencer collaborations.

2. Make Goals Measurable

- **Quantitative Metrics**: Use specific metrics such as reach (impressions), engagement (likes, comments, and shares), click-through rates (CTRs), conversions, and return on investment (ROI).
- **Qualitative Insights**: Assess audience sentiment, brand perception, and qualitative feedback from influencer campaigns.

3. Align with Business Objectives

- **Marketing Alignment**: Ensure influencer marketing goals align with broader marketing objectives, such as increasing sales, enhancing brand loyalty, or entering new markets.
- **Business Impact**: Tie influencer marketing outcomes to business outcomes, demonstrating how campaigns contribute to overall growth and profitability.

4. Set Realistic and Time-Bound Targets

- **SMART Goals**: Ensure goals are Specific, Measurable, Achievable, Relevant, and Time-bound.
- **Timeline**: Establish clear timelines and deadlines for achieving each goal, considering campaign durations, seasonal factors, and market trends.

5. Example of Clear Goals and Objectives

- **Goal**: Increase brand awareness among millennials in urban areas by 20% within six months.
- **Objective**: Collaborate with micro-influencers on Instagram and TikTok to generate 1 million impressions per month.
- **Goal**: Drive a 15% increase in online sales for a new product line within three months.
- **Objective**: Partner with macro-influencers to create engaging content highlighting product features and benefits, with a target of 5% conversion rate from influencer-driven traffic.

Setting clear goals and objectives is the first step in crafting a strategic influencer marketing plan. By defining specific, measurable, and aligned goals, brands can effectively leverage influencer partnerships to achieve desired outcomes, enhance brand visibility, engage with target audiences, and drive meaningful business results. Regular evaluation and adjustment of goals based on campaign performance ensure continuous improvement and optimization of influencer marketing efforts.

4.2 Budgeting and Resource Allocation

Budgeting and resource allocation are critical components of an effective influencer marketing strategy, ensuring that campaigns are executed efficiently and achieve desired outcomes. Here's a detailed approach to setting budgets and allocating resources for influencer marketing:

1. Define Your Influencer Marketing Budget

- **Allocate Resources**: Determine the total budget available for influencer marketing initiatives, considering costs for influencer fees, content creation, campaign management tools, and analytics.
- **Benchmarking**: Research industry standards and competitor spending to set a realistic budget aligned with your campaign goals and expected outcomes.
- **Scalability**: Plan for scalability by allocating resources based on the scope and scale of influencer partnerships, from micro-influencers to mega-influencers.

2. Calculate Influencer Fees

- **Types of Influencers**: Understand the cost range associated with different types of influencers (mega, macro, micro, nano) based on their reach, engagement rates, and industry relevance.
- **Negotiation**: Negotiate influencer fees based on deliverables, exclusivity, campaign duration, and the influencer's market rates. Consider offering additional incentives such as product samples, exclusive access, or long-term partnerships.

3. Resource Allocation

- **Content Creation**: Allocate resources for creating high-quality content that aligns with your brand messaging and resonates with the influencer's audience.
- **Campaign Management**: Invest in tools and platforms for influencer discovery, relationship management, content scheduling, and performance tracking.
- **Legal and Compliance**: Allocate resources for legal considerations, including contracts, disclosures, and compliance with advertising regulations (e.g., FTC guidelines).

4. Optimize Budget Allocation

- **Performance Analysis**: Analyze past campaign performance to identify effective budget allocation strategies and optimize resource distribution for future campaigns.

- **Testing and Iteration**: Allocate a portion of the budget for testing new influencer partnerships, content formats, and campaign strategies to optimize ROI and engagement metrics.

5. Budget Breakdown Example

- **Total Budget**: $50,000 for a quarter-long influencer marketing campaign.
- **Influencer Fees**: Allocate $30,000 for collaborating with a mix of micro, macro, and nano influencers across Instagram, YouTube, and TikTok.
- **Content Creation**: Allocate $10,000 for producing high-quality photos, videos, and sponsored posts aligned with campaign objectives.
- **Campaign Management**: Allocate $5,000 for using influencer marketing platforms, analytics tools, and managing campaign logistics.
- **Miscellaneous**: Reserve $5,000 for unforeseen expenses, legal fees, and additional incentives for influencers.

Effective budgeting and resource allocation are crucial for maximizing the impact of influencer marketing campaigns. By defining a clear budget, calculating influencer fees, allocating resources for content creation and campaign management, and optimizing budget allocation based on performance analysis, brands can execute influencer partnerships strategically and achieve measurable business goals. Regular evaluation and adjustment of budgeting strategies ensure efficient use of resources and continuous improvement in influencer marketing effectiveness.

4.3 Crafting a Compelling Brand Message

Crafting a compelling brand message is essential for influencer marketing campaigns to resonate with audiences authentically and drive meaningful engagement. Here's how to create a compelling brand message that aligns with your campaign goals and captures the attention of your target audience:

1. Understand Your Brand Identity

- **Core Values**: Define your brand's mission, values, and unique selling propositions (USPs) that differentiate your products or services in the market.
- **Brand Voice**: Establish a consistent brand voice that reflects your personality, tone, and style across all communication channels.

2. Define Campaign Objectives

- **Clear Goals**: Align your brand message with specific campaign objectives, such as increasing brand awareness, driving sales, or launching new products.
- **Audience Insights**: Use audience demographics, behaviors, and preferences to tailor your message effectively to resonate with your target audience.

3. Identify Key Messaging Points

- **Value Proposition**: Clearly articulate the benefits and value your brand offers to consumers. Highlight what sets your brand apart from competitors.
- **Key Features**: Focus on key product or service features that address consumer pain points or fulfill specific needs in the marketplace.

4. Tailor Messages for Influencer Partnerships

- **Personalization**: Customize your brand message to fit seamlessly with the influencer's content style, audience preferences, and platform nuances.
- **Relevance**: Ensure that the brand message feels relevant and authentic within the context of the influencer's content and audience expectations.

5. Emphasize Authenticity and Transparency

- **Authenticity**: Keep your brand message authentic by aligning it with genuine experiences, values, and stories that resonate with both the influencer and their audience.
- **Transparency**: Disclose any sponsored relationships transparently to maintain trust and credibility with the audience, adhering to FTC guidelines and best practices.

6. Create Engaging Visual and Written Content

- **Visual Appeal**: Use high-quality images, videos, and graphics that visually represent your brand's message and resonate with the influencer's aesthetic.
- **Compelling Copy**: Craft compelling headlines, captions, and call-to-actions (CTAs) that reinforce your brand message and encourage audience engagement.

7. Consistency across Platforms

- **Multi-platform Alignment**: Ensure consistency in your brand message across various social media platforms and digital channels where influencers are active.
- **Adaptation**: Tailor your message format and style to fit the platform's norms and audience preferences, whether it's Instagram, YouTube, TikTok, or others.

8. Test and Iterate

- **Feedback Loop**: Gather feedback from influencers, monitor audience reactions, and analyze performance metrics to refine and optimize your brand message over time.
- **A/B Testing**: Experiment with different messaging variations, content formats, and campaign strategies to identify what resonates most effectively with your target audience.

9. Measure Impact and Adjust

- **Performance Metrics**: Track key performance indicators (KPIs) such as engagement rates, click-through rates (CTRs), conversions, and sentiment analysis to assess the impact of your brand message.
- **Continuous Improvement**: Use data-driven insights to make informed decisions, optimize messaging strategies, and enhance campaign effectiveness for future influencer collaborations.

Crafting a compelling brand message for influencer marketing involves aligning your brand identity with campaign objectives, tailoring messages to fit influencer partnerships, emphasizing authenticity and transparency, creating engaging content, ensuring consistency across platforms, and continuously testing and refining strategies based on performance metrics. By focusing on clarity, relevance, authenticity, and audience engagement, brands can effectively leverage influencer partnerships to enhance brand perception, drive consumer action, and achieve measurable business growth in today's competitive digital landscape.

4.4 Creating a Content Plan and Timeline

Creating a well-defined content plan and timeline is crucial for executing a successful influencer marketing campaign that aligns with your brand goals and engages your target audience effectively. Here's how to create a comprehensive content plan and timeline for your influencer marketing initiatives:

1. **Set Campaign Objectives and Goals**

- **Clarity**: Define clear and specific campaign objectives, such as increasing brand awareness, driving sales, or launching new products/services.
- **Measurable Goals**: Establish measurable goals that align with your overall marketing strategy, such as achieving a specific number of impressions, engagement rates, or conversions.

2. **Identify Target Audience and Platform Preferences**

- **Audience Segmentation**: Understand your target audience's demographics, behaviors, interests, and preferences to tailor content effectively.
- **Platform Selection**: Choose social media platforms (e.g., Instagram, YouTube, TikTok) where your target audience is most active and engaged with influencers.

3. **Collaborate with Influencers on Content Creation**

- **Content Strategy**: Work closely with influencers to develop a content strategy that aligns with your brand message, campaign goals, and the influencer's content style.
- **Content Formats**: Determine the types of content to be created, such as photos, videos, stories, tutorials, reviews, or live streams, based on audience preferences and platform capabilities.

4. **Develop a Content Calendar**

- **Timeline**: Create a detailed timeline that outlines key milestones, deliverables, and deadlines for content creation, review, and publication.
- **Frequency**: Determine the frequency and timing of influencer posts to optimize reach, engagement, and audience response.

5. **Content Plan Components**

- **Campaign Theme**: Define a cohesive campaign theme or message that ties all content together and reinforces your brand's key messaging points.
- **Content Briefs**: Provide influencers with clear content briefs, including creative guidelines, brand assets, product information, key talking points, and desired calls-to-action (CTAs).

6. **Include Engagement Strategies**

- **Interactive Elements**: Incorporate interactive elements such as polls, quizzes, giveaways, or contests to encourage audience participation and engagement.
- **Community Management**: Plan for ongoing community management to respond to audience comments, questions, and feedback promptly.

7. **Adaptability and Flexibility**

    - **Real-Time Optimization**: Remain flexible to adjust the content plan based on influencer and audience feedback, platform updates, and real-time campaign performance data.
    - **Contingency Planning**: Prepare contingency plans for unforeseen events or changes in campaign dynamics that may impact content scheduling or messaging.

8. **Legal and Compliance Considerations**

    - **Disclosures**: Ensure influencers adhere to FTC guidelines and disclose sponsored content transparently to maintain trust and compliance.
    - **Contracts**: Formalize agreements with influencers, outlining content deliverables, usage rights, compensation terms, and compliance with advertising regulations.

9. **Measurement and Evaluation**

    - **Performance Metrics**: Define key performance indicators (KPIs) to measure the success of the content plan, such as engagement rates, click-through rates (CTRs), conversions, and sentiment analysis.
    - **Analytics Tools**: Utilize analytics tools to track and analyze campaign performance in real time, enabling adjustments and optimizations as needed.

10. **Post-Campaign Analysis and Iteration**

    - **Learning and Optimization**: Conduct a post-campaign analysis to evaluate content performance against campaign goals, gather insights, and identify areas for improvement.
    - **Iterative Improvements**: Apply learnings to refine future content plans, optimize strategies, and enhance the effectiveness of influencer marketing efforts.

Creating a structured content plan and timeline for influencer marketing involves setting clear objectives, collaborating with influencers on content creation, developing a detailed content calendar, incorporating engagement strategies, ensuring legal compliance, and measuring performance effectively. By maintaining flexibility, adapting to audience feedback, and continuously optimizing content strategies based on analytics insights, brands can execute impactful influencer campaigns that resonate with audiences, drive engagement, and achieve tangible business outcomes in today's competitive digital landscape.

4.5 Metrics and KPIs for Measuring Success

Metrics and Key Performance Indicators (KPIs) are essential for evaluating the effectiveness of influencer marketing campaigns and measuring their impact on business objectives. Here's a guide to selecting relevant metrics and KPIs to measure success:

1. **Reach and Impressions**

   - **Metric**: Total reach and impressions generated by influencer posts across social media platforms.
   - **Importance**: Indicates the potential audience exposed to your brand message and content.

2. **Engagement Rates**

   - **Metric**: Likes, comments, shares, and other interactions on influencer posts.
   - **Importance**: Reflects audience engagement levels and the effectiveness of content in capturing attention and encouraging interaction.

3. **Click-Through Rate (CTR)**

   - **Metric**: Percentage of viewers who clicked on a link or CTA in influencer content.
   - **Importance**: Measures the effectiveness of driving traffic from influencer posts to your website or landing pages.

4. **Conversion Rate**

   - **Metric**: Percentage of users who completed a desired action, such as making a purchase or signing up, after clicking on an influencer-generated link.

- **Importance**: Indicates the campaign's ability to convert engaged audiences into customers or leads.

5. **Audience Sentiment and Brand Perception**

- **Metric**: Qualitative feedback, comments, and sentiment analysis from the audience in response to influencer content.
- **Importance**: Provides insights into how the campaign impacts brand perception, sentiment, and audience attitudes towards your brand.

6. **Return on Investment (ROI)**

- **Metric**: Ratio of the campaign's net profit (or revenue) to its total costs, expressed as a percentage.
- **Importance**: Measures the financial impact and profitability of the influencer marketing campaign relative to the investment made.

7. **Follower Growth and Acquisition**

- **Metric**: Increase in followers or subscribers on social media channels as a result of influencer collaborations.
- **Importance**: Indicates the campaign's ability to expand brand reach and attract new audiences to your social media profiles.

8. **Content Performance**

    - **Metric**: Performance of specific content types (e.g., photos, videos, stories) created by influencers.
    - **Importance**: Helps identify which content formats resonate best with the audience and drive higher engagement rates.

9. **Brand Mentions and Hashtag Usage**

    - **Metric**: Number of times your brand is mentioned or associated hashtags are used in influencer content and audience interactions.
    - **Importance**: Measures brand visibility, awareness, and the spread of campaign messaging across social media platforms.

10. **Influencer Effectiveness**

    - **Metric**: Influencer-specific metrics such as follower engagement rates, content quality, and audience demographics.
    - **Importance**: Evaluate the individual influencer's impact on campaign performance and audience engagement.

Selecting the right metrics and KPIs for influencer marketing campaigns is crucial for assessing performance, optimizing strategies, and demonstrating return on investment (ROI). By tracking reach, engagement rates, conversions, audience sentiment, and other relevant metrics, brands can effectively measure the success of their influencer collaborations, refine content strategies, and achieve business objectives in today's dynamic digital landscape. Regular monitoring, analysis of campaign data, and adaptation of strategies based on insights ensure continuous improvement and maximize the impact of influencer marketing efforts.

Chapter 5: Executing Influencer Campaigns

Executing influencer campaigns involves meticulous planning, strategic collaboration, and proactive management to ensure seamless integration of brand messages and effective engagement with target audiences. This chapter delves into key considerations and steps for successfully executing influencer marketing campaigns.

1. Campaign Planning and Preparation

Before launching an influencer campaign, thorough planning is essential. Begin by defining campaign objectives, identifying target audiences, and selecting suitable influencers whose values and audience demographics align with your brand. Establish clear goals such as increasing brand awareness, driving sales, or promoting new products/services, and outline specific KPIs to measure success.

2. Influencer Selection and Collaboration

Choose influencers based on relevance, engagement rates, content quality, and audience authenticity. Initiate collaboration by communicating campaign goals, brand guidelines, and content expectations. Work closely with influencers to develop creative concepts, content themes, and posting schedules that resonate with their audience while aligning with your brand message.

3. Content Creation and Approval

Collaborate with influencers on content creation, ensuring it reflects your brand's values, messaging, and campaign objectives. Provide influencers with necessary brand assets, product information, and key talking points. Review and approve content drafts to maintain brand consistency and compliance with legal guidelines and advertising regulations.

4. Campaign Launch and Management

Coordinate the campaign launch across chosen platforms, ensuring content goes live according to the agreed-upon schedule. Monitor influencer posts and audience interactions closely, engaging with comments, questions, and feedback promptly to foster community engagement and address any concerns. Use campaign management tools and analytics platforms to track real-time performance metrics such as reach, engagement rates, and conversion metrics.

5. Community Engagement and Interaction

Encourage influencers to actively engage with their audience through interactive content formats, polls, Q&A sessions, giveaways, or live streams. Monitor audience sentiment and responses to gauge the effectiveness of content in generating interest, fostering trust, and influencing purchasing decisions.

6. Performance Monitoring and Optimization

Continuously monitor campaign performance against predefined KPIs and benchmarks. Analyze data insights to identify successful strategies, optimize content performance, and refine campaign tactics as needed. Adjust budget allocations, content strategies, or influencer partnerships based on performance data to maximize ROI and achieve campaign objectives effectively.

7. Legal Compliance and Disclosure

Ensure compliance with legal regulations and industry guidelines, such as FTC requirements for disclosing sponsored content. Review and approve influencer disclosures to maintain transparency and credibility with the audience. Use contracts or agreements to formalize partnerships, outline deliverables, and protect both parties' rights throughout the campaign duration.

8. Post-Campaign Evaluation and Analysis

Conduct a comprehensive post-campaign evaluation to assess overall campaign performance, measure ROI, and gather feedback from influencers and stakeholders. Evaluate the impact on brand awareness, audience engagement, and sales conversions. Identify key learnings, successes, and areas for improvement to inform future influencer marketing strategies and optimize campaign outcomes.

Executing influencer campaigns requires careful planning, proactive management, and strategic collaboration to leverage the influence of trusted voices and engage audiences authentically. By focusing on clear objectives, effective influencer selection, collaborative content creation, rigorous campaign management, and continuous performance optimization, brands can maximize the impact of influencer partnerships and achieve measurable business growth in today's competitive digital landscape. Regular evaluation, adaptation of strategies, and adherence to legal and ethical standards ensure sustainable success and long-term benefits from influencer marketing initiatives.

Chapter 5: Executing Influencer Campaigns

Executing influencer campaigns involves meticulous planning, strategic collaboration, and proactive management to ensure seamless integration of brand messages and effective engagement with target audiences. This chapter delves into key considerations and steps for successfully executing influencer marketing campaigns.

Designing Effective Campaigns

Designing an effective influencer campaign hinges on strategic planning, creative execution, and seamless integration of brand messaging with influencer content. Here's a detailed approach to designing campaigns that resonate with audiences and achieve campaign objectives:

1. **Define Clear Campaign Objectives**

Start by clearly defining the campaign's objectives. Whether the goal is to increase brand awareness, drive sales, promote a new product launch, or enhance brand perception, establishing specific and measurable objectives provides direction and benchmarks for success.

2. **Audience Segmentation and Targeting**

Understand your target audience's demographics, behaviors, interests, and preferences. Segment your audience to tailor content and influencer selection effectively. Identify which social media platforms your audience frequents and where influencer impact is most significant.

3. Influencer Selection Criteria

Choose influencers whose values, content style, and audience align closely with your brand. Consider factors such as engagement rates, authenticity, relevance to your industry, and past collaborations. Engage influencers who can authentically convey your brand message to their audience.

4. Collaborative Content Strategy

Work closely with influencers to develop a cohesive content strategy. Align campaign themes, messaging, and creative concepts with your brand guidelines and campaign objectives. Provide influencers with creative freedom within brand parameters to ensure authentic and engaging content.

5. Creative Briefs and Content Development

Develop detailed creative briefs outlining campaign goals, key messages, content formats, and posting schedules. Include brand assets, product information, and any specific requirements. Review and approve content drafts to maintain brand consistency and compliance with legal guidelines.

6. **Execution and Launch**

Coordinate the campaign launch across chosen platforms. Ensure content goes live according to the agreed-upon schedule and integrates seamlessly with influencers' regular content. Monitor influencer posts and audience interactions closely to respond promptly and foster engagement.

7. **Engagement Strategies**

Encourage influencers to engage actively with their audience through interactive content formats, polls, Q&A sessions, giveaways, or live streams. Foster genuine interactions and dialogue that resonate with the audience and reinforce campaign messaging.

8. **Performance Monitoring and Optimization**

Continuously monitor campaign performance using analytics tools. Track key metrics such as reach, engagement rates, click-through rates (CTR), conversion rates, and audience sentiment. Analyze data insights to optimize content performance and adjust campaign strategies as needed.

9. **Compliance and Transparency**

Ensure compliance with legal regulations and industry guidelines, such as FTC requirements for disclosing sponsored content. Review and approve influencer disclosures to maintain transparency and credibility with the audience.

10. Evaluation and Iteration

Conduct a thorough post-campaign evaluation to assess overall performance against objectives. Measure ROI, gather feedback from influencers, and analyze audience feedback. Identify successes, challenges, and areas for improvement to inform future campaigns and optimize outcomes.

Designing and executing effective influencer campaigns requires strategic planning, collaborative efforts with influencers, creative content development, rigorous campaign management, and continuous performance optimization. By focusing on clear objectives, audience targeting, authentic engagement, compliance with legal standards, and data-driven insights, brands can leverage influencer partnerships to enhance brand visibility, drive engagement, and achieve measurable business growth in today's competitive digital landscape. Regular evaluation and adaptation of strategies ensure sustainable success and maximize the impact of influencer marketing initiatives.

5.1 Designing Effective Campaigns

Designing effective influencer campaigns involves a strategic approach that integrates brand goals with influencer creativity and audience engagement. Here's a comprehensive guide to crafting campaigns that resonate and deliver results:

Understanding Campaign Objectives

Begin by clearly defining the objectives of your influencer campaign. Whether it's to increase brand awareness, drive sales, launch a new product, or build brand credibility, setting specific and measurable goals is crucial. This provides a clear direction for all campaign activities.

Audience Research and Segmentation

Conduct thorough research to understand your target audience's demographics, interests, behaviors, and preferences. Segment your audience to tailor campaign messaging and influencer selection effectively. Identify which social media platforms your audience engages with most frequently.

Selecting the Right Influencers

Choose influencers whose values, content style, and audience align closely with your brand's identity and target audience. Consider factors such as engagement rates, authenticity, relevance to your industry, and previous collaborations. Collaborate with influencers who can authentically represent your brand.

Collaborative Content Strategy

Work closely with influencers to develop a cohesive content strategy that aligns with your brand's messaging and campaign objectives.

Provide influencers with creative freedom within brand guidelines to ensure authenticity and resonance with their audience.

Creative Brief Development

Develop detailed creative briefs outlining campaign goals, key messages, content formats, and posting schedules. Include brand assets, product information, and any specific requirements. Review and approve content drafts to maintain consistency and compliance with legal guidelines.

Execution and Monitoring

Coordinate the campaign launch across chosen platforms, ensuring that content integrates seamlessly with influencers' regular posts. Monitor influencer activities and audience interactions closely. Engage with comments, questions, and feedback promptly to foster community engagement.

Measurement and Optimization

Utilize analytics tools to track and measure key performance indicators (KPIs) such as reach, engagement rates, click-through rates (CTR), conversion rates, and sentiment analysis. Analyze data insights to optimize campaign performance and refine strategies in real time.

Compliance and Transparency

Ensure compliance with legal regulations and industry guidelines, including FTC requirements for disclosing sponsored content. Review and approve influencer disclosures to maintain transparency and credibility with the audience.

Evaluation and Iteration

Conduct a thorough post-campaign evaluation to assess overall performance against objectives. Measure ROI, gather feedback from influencers, and analyze audience responses. Identify successful strategies, challenges, and areas for improvement to inform future campaigns and maximize outcomes.

Designing effective influencer campaigns requires strategic planning, collaboration with influencers, creative content development, rigorous monitoring, and continuous optimization based on data-driven insights. By focusing on clear objectives, audience understanding, authentic engagement, compliance, and evaluation, brands can leverage influencer partnerships to enhance brand visibility, drive engagement, and achieve tangible business growth in today's competitive digital landscape.

5.2 Negotiating Contracts and Agreements

Negotiating contracts and agreements with influencers is a critical aspect of executing successful influencer campaigns. Here's a detailed guide to navigating this process effectively:

1. **Define the Scope of Work**

   - **Campaign Objectives**: Clearly outline the goals, deliverables, and timeline of the influencer campaign. Specify whether the collaboration is for a one-time promotion or a long-term partnership.
   - **Content Requirements**: Detail the types of content (e.g., posts, stories, videos) expected from the influencer, including frequency, format, and any creative guidelines.

2. **Compensation and Payment Terms**

   - **Fee Structure**: Determine the influencer's compensation structure, whether it's a flat fee, commission-based, product exchange, or a combination.
   - **Payment Schedule**: Agree on payment terms, including when and how influencers will be compensated (e.g., upfront, milestone-based, post-campaign).

3. **Content Usage Rights**

   - **Usage Rights**: Specify the rights for using influencer-created content, including where and how the brand can use it (e.g., social media, website, and advertising).
   - **Exclusivity**: Clarify exclusivity terms, such as whether the influencer can work with competitors during and after the campaign period.

4. **Disclosure and Compliance**

   - **FTC Guidelines**: Ensure compliance with FTC guidelines by including clear disclosures of sponsored content and partnerships.
   - **Legal Compliance**: Address legal considerations, including intellectual property rights, confidentiality, and liability limitations.

5. **Performance Metrics and Deliverables**

   - **Key Performance Indicators (KPIs)**: Define metrics for measuring campaign success, such as reach, engagement rates, click-through rates (CTR), and conversions.
   - **Deliverables**: Detail-specific deliverables expected from the influencer, including content drafts, publishing schedules, and post-campaign reporting.

6. **Contract Negotiation Tips**

   - **Negotiate Fairly**: Ensure terms are fair and mutually beneficial for both parties, considering the influencer's audience reach, engagement rates, and industry standards.
   - **Flexibility**: Be open to negotiations on terms like exclusivity, content revisions, and payment schedules to accommodate both parties' needs.

7. Legal Review and Approval

- **Consult Legal Expertise**: If necessary, seek legal counsel to review and approve contracts to protect both parties' rights and ensure compliance with local laws.

8. Clear Communication and Documentation

- **Written Agreement**: Document all agreed-upon terms in a written contract or agreement signed by both parties.
- **Communication Channels**: Establish clear communication channels for ongoing collaboration, feedback, and revisions throughout the campaign.

9. Relationship Management

- **Build Rapport**: Foster a positive relationship with influencers based on transparency, respect, and professionalism.
- **Support**: Provide influencers with necessary resources, brand assets, and support to ensure they can deliver quality content aligned with campaign objectives.

10. Continuous Evaluation and Feedback

- **Performance Review**: Regularly review campaign performance against KPIs, gather feedback from influencers, and iterate strategies for future collaborations.

Negotiating contracts and agreements with influencers requires careful planning, clear communication, and a thorough understanding of campaign objectives and legal considerations. By defining scope, compensation, content rights, compliance, and performance metrics upfront, brands can establish mutually beneficial partnerships that drive engagement, enhance brand visibility, and achieve measurable business results through influencer marketing campaigns. Regular evaluation, flexibility in negotiations, and adherence to ethical standards ensure successful and sustainable influencer collaborations in today's dynamic digital landscape.

5.3 Best Practices for Collaboration and Communication

Effective collaboration and communication with influencers are crucial for the success of influencer marketing campaigns. Building strong relationships with influencers can lead to more authentic and impactful content that resonates with your target audience. Here are the best practices for fostering successful partnerships with influencers:

1. **Establish Clear Communication Channels**

- **Primary Contact**: Designate a primary point of contact for the influencer to streamline communication and ensure consistency.
- **Preferred Platforms**: Use the influencer's preferred communication platforms (e.g., email, and messaging apps) to facilitate smooth interactions.

2. Set Clear Expectations and Guidelines

- **Campaign Brief**: Provide a detailed campaign brief outlining objectives, key messages, target audience, and content requirements.
- **Creative Freedom**: Allow influencers creative freedom within the provided guidelines to ensure authenticity and alignment with their brand.

3. Regular and Transparent Communication

- **Kick-off Meetings**: Hold initial meetings to discuss campaign goals, timelines, and expectations, ensuring both parties are aligned.
- **Ongoing Updates**: Maintain regular check-ins to provide updates, gather feedback, and address any concerns promptly.

4. Provide Comprehensive Resources

- **Brand Assets**: Supply influencers with brand assets, including logos, product information, style guides, and key talking points.
- **Support Materials**: Offer any additional resources that may help influencers create high-quality content, such as product samples or access to brand experts.

5. **Foster Authentic Relationships**

   - **Personal Connection**: Invest time in building personal relationships with influencers to understand their motivations, values, and creative processes.
   - **Recognition and Appreciation**: Show appreciation for influencers' efforts and contributions through public acknowledgments, thank-you notes, or additional incentives.

6. **Collaborative Content Development**

   - **Brainstorming Sessions**: Involve influencers in the content creation process through collaborative brainstorming sessions to generate creative ideas.
   - **Feedback Loop**: Establish a feedback loop where influencers can share drafts and receive constructive feedback to refine their content.

7. **Flexibility and Adaptability**

   - **Adapt to Changes**: Be flexible and adaptable to changes in campaign dynamics, influencer availability, or audience feedback.
   - **Real-Time Adjustments**: Allow for real-time adjustments to content or strategy based on performance data and insights.

8. Ensure Legal and Ethical Compliance

- **FTC Guidelines**: Ensure influencers adhere to FTC guidelines and disclose sponsored content transparently.
- **Contracts and Agreements**: Formalize agreements with detailed contracts outlining roles, responsibilities, deliverables, and compliance requirements.

9. Monitor Performance and Provide Feedback

- **Performance Tracking**: Use analytics tools to monitor campaign performance against predefined KPIs.
- **Constructive Feedback**: Provide constructive feedback based on performance data to help influencers improve and optimize their content.

10. Post-Campaign Evaluation and Relationship Building

- **Post-Campaign Review**: Conduct a thorough post-campaign review to evaluate success, gather insights, and identify areas for improvement.
- **Long-Term Relationships**: Invest in building long-term relationships with influencers by offering future collaboration opportunities and maintaining regular contact.

Effective collaboration and communication with influencers are fundamental to executing successful influencer marketing campaigns.

By establishing clear communication channels, setting expectations, fostering authentic relationships, and ensuring legal compliance, brands can create a supportive and productive environment for influencers. Regular performance monitoring, constructive feedback, and flexibility in adapting to changes enhance the overall campaign effectiveness. Building long-term relationships with influencers not only leads to more impactful campaigns but also strengthens brand loyalty and authenticity in the eyes of the audience.

5.4 Monitoring and Optimizing Campaign Performance

Monitoring and optimizing campaign performance are essential steps to ensure the success and effectiveness of influencer marketing efforts. This involves continuous tracking, analysis, and adjustments based on data-driven insights to maximize return on investment (ROI) and achieve campaign objectives.

1. **Establish Key Performance Indicators (KPIs)**

   - **Define Clear KPIs**: Identify specific metrics that align with campaign objectives, such as reach, engagement rates, click-through rates (CTR), conversion rates, and return on investment (ROI).
   - **Set Benchmarks**: Establish benchmarks and performance targets based on industry standards, previous campaigns, or competitive analysis.

2. **Utilize Analytics Tools**

   - **Social Media Analytics**: Use platform-specific analytics tools (e.g., Instagram Insights, YouTube Analytics) to track performance metrics in real time.
   - **Third-Party Tools**: Leverage third-party analytics platforms (e.g., Google Analytics, Hootsuite, and Sprout Social) for comprehensive data collection and analysis across multiple channels.

3. **Track Real-Time Performance**

   - **Content Monitoring**: Monitor influencer content as it goes live to ensure it meets brand guidelines and resonates with the audience.
   - **Engagement Tracking**: Track real-time engagement metrics such as likes, comments, shares, and mentions to gauge audience response and interaction.

4. **Analyze Campaign Data**

   - **Data Collection**: Collect quantitative and qualitative data throughout the campaign, including audience demographics, engagement patterns, and sentiment analysis.
   - **Performance Analysis**: Analyze data to identify trends, strengths, and areas for improvement. Compare performance against benchmarks and KPIs to assess effectiveness.

5. **Adjust and Optimize Strategy**

   - **Identify Opportunities**: Use data insights to identify opportunities for optimization, such as high-performing content types, optimal posting times, and effective messaging.
   - **Make Real-Time Adjustments**: Adjust campaign elements in real-time based on performance data, such as tweaking content, changing posting schedules, or reallocating budget.

6. **Engage with the Audience**

   - **Community Management**: Actively engage with the audience by responding to comments, messages, and feedback on influencer posts.
   - **Audience Feedback**: Gather and analyze audience feedback to understand their perceptions, preferences, and areas of interest.

7. **Collaborate with Influencers**

   - **Ongoing Communication**: Maintain open lines of communication with influencers to discuss performance insights, gather their feedback, and make collaborative adjustments.
   - **Feedback Loop**: Establish a feedback loop where influencers can share their observations and suggest improvements based on their audience interactions.

8. Report and Share Results

- **Comprehensive Reporting**: Create detailed campaign performance reports that include key metrics, insights, and visual representations of data.
- **Stakeholder Communication**: Share results with stakeholders, including marketing teams, executives, and influencers, to demonstrate campaign impact and inform future strategies.

9. Post-Campaign Evaluation

- **Evaluate Success**: Conduct a thorough post-campaign evaluation to measure overall success against objectives and KPIs.
- **Lessons Learned**: Identify key takeaways, successes, and challenges to inform future campaigns and improve strategies.

10. Continuous Improvement

- **Iterative Approach**: Adopt an iterative approach to influencer marketing, continuously refining strategies based on data-driven insights and evolving industry trends.
- **Training and Development**: Invest in training and development for your marketing team to stay updated on the latest tools, techniques, and best practices in influencer marketing.

Monitoring and optimizing campaign performance is crucial for maximizing the impact and ROI of influencer marketing campaigns. By establishing clear KPIs, utilizing analytics tools, tracking real-time performance, and making data-driven adjustments, brands can ensure their campaigns are effective and aligned with objectives. Engaging with the audience, collaborating with influencers, and conducting thorough post-campaign evaluations provide valuable insights for continuous improvement. A proactive and iterative approach to monitoring and optimization helps brands stay competitive and achieve sustainable success in influencer marketing.

Chapter 6: Legal and Ethical Considerations

Navigating the legal and ethical landscape of influencer marketing is crucial for maintaining brand integrity, complying with regulations, and fostering trust with audiences. This chapter explores the key legal requirements and ethical practices necessary for conducting responsible influencer marketing campaigns.

1. Understanding Legal Requirements

Influencer marketing operates within a framework of legal guidelines designed to protect consumers and ensure transparency. Key legal requirements include:

Federal Trade Commission (FTC) Guidelines

- **Disclosure of Sponsored Content**: Influencers must disclose when content is sponsored or when there is a material connection between the influencer and the brand. This includes using hashtags like #ad, #sponsored, or clear language such as "This post is sponsored by [Brand]."
- **Honesty and Accuracy**: Influencers must provide honest and accurate representations of products and services. Misleading claims or false endorsements can lead to legal repercussions.

Intellectual Property Rights

- **Content Ownership**: Clearly define who owns the rights to the content created during the campaign. Typically, influencers retain ownership, but brands may negotiate usage rights.
- **Copyright Compliance**: Ensure that all content, including images, music, and videos, does not infringe on third-party copyrights. Proper licenses or permissions must be obtained.

Data Protection and Privacy

- **GDPR Compliance**: For campaigns targeting European audiences, ensure compliance with the General Data Protection Regulation (GDPR). This includes obtaining explicit consent for data collection and providing transparency on data usage.
- **Privacy Policies**: Communicate how user data will be collected, used, and protected. Ensure that privacy policies are accessible and adhered to.

2. Ethical Considerations

Beyond legal compliance, ethical considerations play a vital role in building and maintaining consumer trust. Key ethical practices include:

Transparency and Authenticity

- **Genuine Endorsements**: Encourage influencers to provide genuine endorsements based on their true experiences and opinions. Authenticity is key to maintaining audience trust.
- **Clear Disclosures**: Ensure that disclosures are clear, conspicuous, and easy for the audience to understand. Hidden or ambiguous disclosures undermine trust and can lead to legal issues.

Fair Compensation

- **Fair Payment**: Compensate influencers fairly for their work, considering the time, effort, and reach involved. Avoid exploiting influencers by offering inadequate compensation.
- **Timely Payments**: Adhere to agreed-upon payment schedules to maintain a professional relationship and trust with influencers.

Respect for Audience

- **Truthful Marketing**: Avoid using deceptive marketing practices or exaggerated claims that can mislead the audience.
- **Respect Cultural Sensitivities**: Be mindful of cultural differences and sensitivities when crafting content to avoid offending or alienating audience segments.

3. Contracts and Agreements

Clear, detailed contracts are essential for outlining the terms of collaboration and protecting the interests of both parties. Key components of influencer contracts include:

Scope of Work

- **Deliverables**: Clearly define the content deliverables, including the type, quantity, and format of content to be produced.
- **Timelines**: Specify deadlines for content creation, review, and publication to ensure the timely execution of the campaign.

Compensation and Payment Terms

- **Fee Structure**: Detail the compensation structure, including flat fees, commission, product exchange, or performance-based incentives.
- **Payment Schedule**: Outline when and how payments will be made, such as upfront, milestone-based, or post-campaign.

Usage Rights and Exclusivity

- **Content Usage**: Define how the brand can use the influencer's content, including social media, websites, advertising, and other channels.
- **Exclusivity Clauses**: Specify any exclusivity requirements, such as prohibiting the influencer from working with competitors during and after the campaign.

4. Addressing Potential Issues

Proactively addressing potential legal and ethical issues can prevent problems and enhance campaign success. Consider the following:

Crisis Management

- **Response Plans**: Develop a plan for handling negative feedback, controversies, or legal issues that may arise during the campaign.
- **Communication**: Maintain open communication with influencers to address any concerns promptly and transparently.

Continuous Education

- **Training**: Provide ongoing education and training for marketing teams and influencers on legal requirements, ethical practices, and industry standards.
- **Updates**: Stay informed about changes in regulations and best practices to ensure continuous compliance and ethical conduct.

Legal and ethical considerations are integral to successful and sustainable influencer marketing campaigns. By understanding and adhering to legal requirements, fostering transparency and authenticity, establishing clear contracts, and proactively addressing potential issues, brands can build trust with audiences and create impactful influencer partnerships. Continuous education and vigilance ensure that campaigns not only achieve their objectives but also uphold the highest standards of integrity and responsibility in the digital marketing landscape.

6.1 Understanding FTC Guidelines and Regulations

The Federal Trade Commission (FTC) guidelines and regulations are essential for ensuring transparency and honesty in influencer marketing. These rules protect consumers by requiring clear disclosures of sponsored content and preventing deceptive advertising practices. Understanding and adhering to these guidelines is crucial for brands and influencers alike.

Disclosure of Sponsored Content

The FTC mandates that influencers disclose their relationships with brands when endorsing products or services. This includes any material connections, such as payments, free products, or other compensation. Key points to consider:

- **Clear and Conspicuous Disclosures**: Disclosures must be easy to notice and understand. They should not be hidden in hashtags, small print, or buried within a long list of other hashtags or links. Phrases like "#ad" or "#sponsored" should be used prominently.
- **Proximity to Endorsement**: The disclosure should be placed close to the endorsement message. For example, if an influencer posts a photo of a product on Instagram, the disclosure should be included in the caption where it is easily visible.
- **Plain Language**: Use simple, clear language that the average consumer can easily understand. Avoid ambiguous terms or abbreviations that might confuse the audience.

Honesty and Accuracy

The FTC requires that all endorsements must reflect the honest opinions, findings, beliefs, or experiences of the endorser. Key aspects include:

- **Truthful Representations**: Influencers must provide truthful accounts of their experiences with the product or service. Misleading claims, such as exaggerated benefits or false testimonials, are prohibited.
- **Actual Use of Product**: Influencers should have used the product or service they are endorsing. Claims made about a product should be based on personal experience and not fabricated.

Material Connections

Material connections between influencers and brands must be disclosed if they are not reasonably expected by the audience. These connections can include:

- **Payments**: Any form of monetary compensation, whether a flat fee, commission, or other financial incentives.
- **Free Products or Services**: Receiving free products or services in exchange for an endorsement.
- **Employment Relationships**: Employment or ownership stakes in the company being endorsed.

Guidelines for Different Platforms

The FTC recognizes that different social media platforms have unique features and formats. Therefore, disclosures must be tailored to fit the platform while maintaining transparency:

- **Instagram**: Disclosures should be included in the caption or superimposed on the image or video. Avoid burying disclosures in the middle of a long list of hashtags.
- **YouTube**: Disclosures should be made in the video itself, ideally at the beginning and verbally, as well as in the video description.
- **Twitter**: Due to character limits, short disclosures like "#ad" are acceptable, but they must be placed prominently within the tweet.

Consequences of Non-Compliance

Failure to comply with FTC guidelines can lead to various consequences for both brands and influencers:

- **Legal Action**: The FTC can take legal action against companies and influencers who do not comply with disclosure requirements. This can result in fines, penalties, and mandated corrective actions.
- **Reputation Damage**: Non-compliance can damage the reputation of both the brand and the influencer, leading to a loss of trust among consumers and potential loss of business.

Best Practices for Compliance

To ensure compliance with FTC guidelines, consider the following best practices:

- **Training and Education**: Provide regular training for influencers and marketing teams on FTC guidelines and the importance of transparent disclosures.
- **Contractual Agreements**: Include clear disclosure requirements in contracts with influencers to ensure they understand and comply with FTC regulations.
- **Monitoring and Enforcement**: Regularly monitor influencer content to ensure proper disclosures are made. Take corrective action if non-compliance is detected.

Understanding and adhering to FTC guidelines and regulations is vital for maintaining transparency, building consumer trust, and avoiding legal repercussions in influencer marketing. By ensuring clear and conspicuous disclosures, promoting honesty and accuracy, and managing material connections, brands and influencers can conduct ethical and compliant campaigns. Regular education, contractual clarity, and proactive monitoring further support adherence to these essential guidelines.

6.2 Ensuring Transparency and Authenticity

Transparency and authenticity are fundamental principles in influencer marketing, crucial for building and maintaining trust with audiences.

Ensuring that all aspects of a campaign are transparent and authentic not only complies with legal requirements but also fosters genuine connections between brands, influencers, and their followers.

Transparency in Influencer Marketing

Transparency involves being open and honest about the nature of the relationship between brands and influencers. This includes clear disclosures of sponsored content, honesty about endorsements, and transparency in content creation.

Clear Disclosures

- **Mandatory Disclosures**: Influencers must disclose any material connections with brands, such as payments, free products, or other compensation. This can be done using clear and concise language, like "#ad" or "#sponsored."
- **Placement and Visibility**: Disclosures should be easily visible and placed close to the endorsement message. On social media, this means including the disclosure in the caption or superimposed on the image or video.
- **Consistent Communication**: Ensure that disclosures are made consistently across all platforms and types of content. Whether it's a blog post, a social media update, or a video, the nature of the relationship should always be clear to the audience.

Honesty in Endorsements

- **Truthful Experiences**: Influencers should share their honest experiences and opinions about the products or services they are endorsing. Misleading claims or false testimonials can damage credibility and trust.
- **Actual Use**: Influencers should only endorse products or services they have used and can personally vouch for. This authenticity is crucial for maintaining audience trust.

Content Creation Transparency

- **Behind-the-Scenes Access**: Sharing behind-the-scenes content or the process of creating sponsored content can increase transparency and authenticity. This allows followers to see the effort and creativity involved.
- **Open Communication**: Encourage open communication between brands and influencers during the content creation process. This helps ensure that the final content aligns with both brand values and the influencer's authentic voice.

Authenticity in Influencer Marketing

Authenticity involves genuine endorsements and interactions that resonate with the influencer's audience. It requires maintaining the influencer's unique voice and style while integrating brand messaging naturally.

Genuine Endorsements

- **Personal Stories**: Influencers should share personal stories or experiences related to the product or service. This personal touch makes endorsements more relatable and credible.
- **Audience Relevance**: Ensure that the products or services being promoted are relevant to the influencer's audience. Misaligned endorsements can come across as inauthentic and may alienate followers.

Maintaining Influencer's Voice

- **Creative Freedom**: Allow influencers the creative freedom to present the brand in a way that fits their unique style and voice. Overly scripted or forced content can appear inauthentic and reduce engagement.
- **Natural Integration**: Integrate brand messaging naturally into the influencer's content. The promotion should feel like a seamless part of the influencer's regular content rather than an obvious advertisement.

Long-Term Relationships

- **Ongoing Partnerships**: Building long-term relationships with influencers can lead to more authentic endorsements. Repeated collaborations allow influencers to develop a deeper connection with the brand, resulting in more genuine content.

- **Consistent Messaging**: Long-term partnerships help maintain consistent brand messaging and build stronger, more authentic connections with the audience.

Building Trust with Audiences

Building and maintaining trust is essential for successful influencer marketing. Transparency and authenticity play a significant role in fostering this trust.

Engagement and Interaction

- **Active Engagement**: Encourage influencers to actively engage with their followers, responding to comments, questions, and feedback. This interaction builds a sense of community and trust.
- **Honest Feedback**: Influencers should be open to providing honest feedback about the products or services they endorse, even if it includes constructive criticism. This honesty reinforces their credibility and trustworthiness.

Regular Monitoring

- **Performance Tracking**: Regularly monitor campaign performance and influencer content to ensure compliance with transparency and authenticity standards.

- **Feedback Loop**: Establish a feedback loop with influencers to gather insights and make necessary adjustments to maintain the integrity of the campaign.

Ensuring transparency and authenticity in influencer marketing is vital for building trust, credibility, and long-lasting relationships with audiences. By making clear disclosures, promoting honesty in endorsements, allowing creative freedom, and fostering genuine connections, brands and influencers can create impactful and trustworthy campaigns. Regular engagement, honest feedback, and ongoing monitoring further support these principles, ensuring that influencer marketing efforts are both compliant and effective in today's digital landscape.

6.3 Managing Influencer Relationships and Agreements

Managing influencer relationships and agreements is critical to the success of influencer marketing campaigns. This involves establishing clear contracts, maintaining strong and professional relationships, and ensuring that both parties understand and fulfill their responsibilities. Proper management of these relationships helps ensure smooth campaign execution, compliance with legal requirements, and mutual satisfaction.

Establishing Clear Contracts

Contracts form the foundation of influencer collaborations, outlining the expectations, responsibilities, and terms of the partnership. Key components of a comprehensive influencer contract include:

Scope of Work

- **Deliverables**: Clearly define the type and quantity of content to be created, including specifics like format (e.g., posts, videos), platforms (e.g., Instagram, YouTube), and themes.
- **Content Guidelines**: Provide detailed brand guidelines that include key messages, tone, style, and any specific requirements or restrictions.

Compensation and Payment Terms

- **Fee Structure**: Outline the compensation model, whether it's a flat fee, performance-based payment, commission, or product exchange. Include any bonuses or incentives for achieving specific performance metrics.
- **Payment Schedule**: Specify the payment terms, including when payments will be made (e.g., upfront, milestones, post-campaign) and the method of payment.

Usage Rights and Exclusivity

- **Content Usage**: Define how and where the brand can use the influencer's content. This can include social media, websites, advertising, and other promotional materials.
- **Exclusivity Clauses**: If applicable, include exclusivity terms that prevent the influencer from promoting competing brands during and for a specified period after the campaign.

Legal and Compliance Terms

- **Disclosure Requirements**: Ensure compliance with FTC guidelines by specifying the need for clear and conspicuous disclosures of sponsored content.
- **Termination Clause**: Include terms for terminating the agreement, including conditions under which either party can end the partnership or any associated penalties.

Building Strong Relationships

Strong, professional relationships with influencers are essential for long-term success and can lead to more authentic and impactful collaborations. Best practices for building and maintaining these relationships include:

Clear and Open Communication

- **Regular Check-ins**: Schedule regular check-ins to discuss progress, provide feedback, and address any concerns. This helps keep both parties aligned and ensures the campaign stays on track.
- **Transparency**: Maintain open and honest communication about campaign expectations, performance metrics, and any changes to the campaign plan.

Mutual Respect and Trust

- **Value the Influencer's Input**: Respect the influencer's creative process and expertise. Involve them in brainstorming sessions and value their suggestions and feedback.
- **Timely Responses and Payments**: Respond promptly to the influencer's queries and ensure timely payments as agreed in the contract. This demonstrates professionalism and respect for their work.

Personal Connection

- **Get to Know the Influencer**: Invest time in understanding the influencer's brand, audience, and personal interests. This helps create a more personalized and effective collaboration.
- **Show Appreciation**: Acknowledge the influencer's efforts and achievements, whether through public recognition, thank-you notes, or additional incentives.

Ensuring Compliance and Performance

Monitoring compliance and performance is crucial to ensure that the influencer meets contractual obligations and the campaign achieves its objectives.

Performance Tracking

- **Analytics Tools**: Use analytics tools to track key performance indicators (KPIs) such as reach, engagement, click-through rates, and conversions. Regularly review these metrics to assess campaign effectiveness.
- **Feedback Loop**: Establish a feedback loop to gather insights from both the brand and the influencer. Use this feedback to make real-time adjustments and optimize performance.

Compliance Monitoring

- **Disclosure Checks**: Regularly check that the influencer is making the required disclosures according to FTC guidelines. Address any non-compliance issues promptly.
- **Content Review**: Review the content to ensure it aligns with brand guidelines and campaign objectives. Provide constructive feedback and support to help the influencer meet expectations.

Conflict Resolution

- **Address Issues Promptly**: If issues arise, address them promptly and professionally. Clear communication and a cooperative approach can resolve most conflicts.
- **Document Resolutions**: Document any agreements or resolutions made during the conflict resolution process to ensure clarity and prevent future misunderstandings.

Managing influencer relationships and agreements effectively is vital for the success of influencer marketing campaigns. Clear contracts establish the foundation for collaboration, outlining expectations, responsibilities, and legal requirements. Building strong, respectful relationships with influencers fosters trust and mutual satisfaction, leading to more authentic and impactful content. Continuous monitoring of compliance and performance ensures that campaigns meet their objectives and adhere to legal standards. By investing in these practices, brands can create successful and sustainable influencer marketing partnerships.

6.4 Ethical Issues in Influencer Marketing

Influencer marketing, while powerful, comes with its set of ethical challenges that must be addressed to maintain trust, credibility, and integrity. Navigating these ethical issues is essential for fostering genuine relationships with audiences and ensuring long-term success in influencer marketing campaigns.

Transparency and Disclosure

Lack of Clear Disclosure

- **Deceptive Practices**: Failing to disclose sponsorships or partnerships can deceive audiences, leading them to believe endorsements are organic rather than paid. This violates FTC guidelines and undermines trust.
- **Proper Disclosure Practices**: Influencers and brands must ensure that sponsorships are disclosed using unambiguous language like

"ad," "sponsored," or "paid partnership." Disclosures should be prominently placed within the content to be easily noticeable.

Hidden Endorsements

- **Misleading Integrations**: Sometimes, sponsored content is integrated so seamlessly that viewers might not realize it's an advertisement. This can be misleading.
- **Explicit Statements**: To avoid this, influencers should explicitly state their relationship with the brand within the content, ensuring viewers are aware of the sponsorship.

Authenticity and Honesty

Misrepresentation of Products

- **Exaggerated Claims**: Making exaggerated or false claims about a product's effectiveness can mislead consumers and damage the brand's reputation.
- **Honest Reviews**: Influencers should provide honest reviews based on their real experiences. Brands should encourage influencers to share both positive and negative aspects to maintain authenticity.

Inauthentic Content

- **Scripted Content**: Overly scripted or forced content can appear inauthentic, leading to a loss of trust. Influencers should have the creative freedom to present the brand in their unique voice.
- **Creative Freedom**: Allow influencers to express their genuine opinions and experiences. Authenticity resonates more with audiences and is more likely to drive engagement and trust.

Audience Exploitation

Targeting Vulnerable Audiences

- **Manipulative Tactics**: Targeting vulnerable audiences, such as children or individuals with low self-esteem, with manipulative marketing tactics is unethical and can cause harm.
- **Responsible Marketing**: Brands and influencers should be mindful of their audience's vulnerability and avoid exploiting them. Marketing messages should be crafted responsibly, with consideration for the audience's well-being.

Invasive Marketing Practices

- **Intrusive Methods**: Using invasive marketing practices, such as excessive posting or overly aggressive promotions, can alienate audiences.
- **Respectful Engagement**: Engage with the audience respectfully, avoiding spammy or intrusive tactics. Quality content and genuine interactions foster better relationships.

Cultural Sensitivity

Cultural Appropriation

- **Insensitive Content**: Using elements from cultures without understanding their significance can be seen as disrespectful and exploitative.
- **Cultural Respect**: Brands and influencers should educate themselves about the cultures they engage with and ensure that content is respectful and appreciative, not appropriative.

Stereotyping and Bias

- **Harmful Stereotypes**: Relying on stereotypes or biased portrayals can perpetuate harmful narratives and alienate segments of the audience.
- **Inclusive Representation**: Strive for inclusive and diverse representation in marketing campaigns, showcasing a broad range of experiences and perspectives without resorting to stereotypes.

Privacy Concerns

Data Privacy Violations

- **Unauthorized Data Use**: Collecting and using audience data without consent violates privacy rights and can lead to legal repercussions.
- **Data Protection Compliance**: Ensure compliance with data protection regulations like GDPR. Obtain explicit consent for data collection and use, and communicate privacy policies transparently.

Influencer Privacy

- **Overexposure**: Pressuring influencers to share more personal information than they are comfortable with can invade their privacy and harm their mental health.
- **Respect Boundaries**: Respect influencers' privacy and boundaries, allowing them to share only what they are comfortable with. This fosters a healthier and more sustainable working relationship.

Fair Compensation and Treatment

Exploitation of Influencers

- **Underpayment**: Offering inadequate compensation for the influencer's work and reach is exploitative and unethical.
- **Fair Payment Practices**: Ensure influencers are fairly compensated for their efforts, considering the time, effort, and resources required to create content. Transparent payment terms should be established upfront.

Unrealistic Expectations

- **Excessive Demands**: Placing unrealistic demands on influencers, such as overly tight deadlines or excessive content requirements, can strain relationships and impact content quality.
- **Reasonable Expectations**: Set reasonable and mutually agreed-upon expectations for deliverables, timelines, and workload to maintain a positive and productive partnership.

Addressing ethical issues in influencer marketing is critical for maintaining trust, credibility, and long-term success. Transparency in disclosures, authenticity in content creation, respectful audience engagement, cultural sensitivity, privacy protection, and fair treatment of influencers are essential practices for ethical influencer marketing. By adhering to these principles, brands and influencers can foster genuine connections with their audiences, uphold their reputations, and achieve sustainable success in their marketing efforts.

Chapter 7: Advanced Strategies and Trends

As influencer marketing continues to evolve, staying ahead of the curve requires leveraging advanced strategies and understanding emerging trends. This chapter explores cutting-edge tactics and highlights the trends that are shaping the future of influencer marketing in 2024 and beyond.

1. Personalization and Hyper-Targeting

In 2024, personalization is more crucial than ever. Audiences expect tailored experiences that resonate with their unique preferences and behaviors. Hyper-targeting, enabled by advanced data analytics and AI, allows brands to create highly personalized content that speaks directly to individual consumers.

Data-Driven Insights

- **Behavioral Analysis**: Utilizing data analytics to understand consumer behaviors, preferences, and purchase patterns. This helps in crafting personalized content that appeals to specific audience segments.
- **AI and Machine Learning**: Leveraging AI and machine learning to analyze vast amounts of data and predict consumer preferences. These technologies can help create highly targeted campaigns that are more likely to convert.

Customized Content

- **Dynamic Content Creation**: Using dynamic content tools to create multiple versions of a campaign tailored to different audience segments. This ensures that each segment receives content that is most relevant to them.
- **Personalized Interactions**: Encouraging influencers to personalize their interactions with followers. This can include addressing followers by name, responding to their comments and messages, and creating content that feels more intimate and personal.

2. Cross-Platform Campaigns

With audiences scattered across various social media platforms, cross-platform campaigns are becoming essential. These campaigns ensure a consistent brand message while leveraging the unique strengths of each platform.

Integrated Marketing

- **Consistent Messaging**: Maintaining a consistent brand message across all platforms, ensuring that the audience receives a cohesive experience regardless of where they encounter the brand.
- **Platform-Specific Strategies**: Adapting content to fit the strengths of each platform. For example, using short, engaging videos on TikTok, in-depth tutorials on YouTube, and visually appealing posts on Instagram.

Omnichannel Presence

- **Seamless Integration**: Creating a seamless experience across different channels, allowing audiences to interact with the brand in multiple ways. This can include integrating social media campaigns with email marketing, websites, and offline events.
- **Unified Analytics**: Using unified analytics tools to track performance across all platforms. This provides a holistic view of the campaign's success and helps in making data-driven decisions.

3. The Rise of Micro and Nano Influencers

Micro and nano influencers, with their highly engaged and loyal followings, are becoming increasingly valuable. These influencers offer a more authentic and relatable voice, often leading to higher engagement rates compared to macro influencers.

High Engagement Rates

- **Niche Audiences**: Micro and nano influencers typically cater to niche audiences, allowing brands to target specific demographics more effectively.
- **Authentic Connections**: These influencers often have closer, more personal connections with their followers, resulting in higher trust and engagement levels.

Cost-Effective Campaigns

- **Budget-Friendly**: Collaborating with micro and nano influencers is often more cost-effective than partnering with macro influencers. This allows brands to work with multiple influencers within the same budget.
- **Scalable Impact**: While individually smaller in reach, the collective impact of several micro and nano influencers can be significant, providing widespread brand exposure.

4. Long-Term Partnerships

Building long-term partnerships with influencers fosters deeper relationships and more authentic content. These ongoing collaborations can enhance brand loyalty and provide more consistent messaging over time.

Brand Ambassadors

- **Continuous Engagement**: Long-term partnerships turn influencers into brand ambassadors who consistently promote the brand, leading to stronger brand recall and loyalty.
- **Deeper Integration**: Ongoing collaborations allow influencers to integrate the brand more naturally into their content, creating more genuine endorsements.

Mutual Growth

- **Shared Goals**: Developing shared goals and strategies that benefit both the brand and the influencer. This includes co-creating content, sharing growth strategies, and collaborating on product development.
- **Feedback and Improvement**: Long-term relationships enable continuous feedback and improvement, allowing both parties to refine their strategies and enhance their performance.

5. Influencer-Generated Products

Collaborating with influencers to create co-branded products is a growing trend. These products often resonate well with the influencer's audience and can drive significant sales and brand awareness.

Co-Creation

- **Collaborative Development**: Working closely with influencers to develop products that reflect their brand and appeal to their audience. This can include limited-edition releases, special collections, or custom-designed items.
- **Unique Offerings**: Creating unique products that stand out in the market and offer something exclusive to the influencer's followers.

Enhanced Credibility

- **Influencer Trust**: Products co-created with trusted influencers carry their endorsement, lending credibility and trust to the brand.
- **Authentic Promotion**: Influencers are more likely to promote products they helped create with genuine enthusiasm, leading to more authentic and effective marketing.

6. The Impact of Emerging Technologies

Emerging technologies such as augmented reality (AR), virtual reality (VR), and blockchain are transforming influencer marketing, offering new ways to engage audiences and enhance campaign effectiveness.

Augmented and Virtual Reality

- **Immersive Experiences**: Using AR and VR to create immersive experiences that allow audiences to interact with products in new and engaging ways. This can include virtual try-ons, AR filters, and VR events.
- **Enhanced Storytelling**: Leveraging these technologies to tell more compelling and interactive stories, providing a deeper connection with the audience.

Blockchain and Transparency

- **Proof of Authenticity**: Using blockchain to verify the authenticity of influencer endorsements and ensure transparency in the partnership. This can help combat issues like fake followers and fraudulent activities.
- **Secure Transactions**: Blockchain can also facilitate secure and transparent payment processes, ensuring that influencers are paid fairly and promptly.

Staying ahead in influencer marketing requires embracing advanced strategies and keeping up with emerging trends. Personalization, cross-platform campaigns, leveraging micro and nano influencers, fostering long-term partnerships, co-creating products, and adopting new technologies are key to maintaining a competitive edge. By continuously innovating and adapting to the evolving landscape, brands can build stronger, more authentic connections with their audiences and drive lasting success in their influencer marketing efforts.

7.1 Leveraging Data and Analytics

In the rapidly evolving world of influencer marketing, leveraging data and analytics is essential for crafting effective strategies, optimizing campaigns, and achieving measurable results. Data-driven insights enable brands to make informed decisions, target the right audiences, and enhance the overall impact of their influencer marketing efforts.

Data-Driven Influencer Selection

Selecting the right influencers is crucial for the success of a campaign. Data and analytics provide valuable insights into influencer performance, audience demographics, and engagement metrics.

Influencer Performance Metrics

- **Engagement Rates**: Analyze influencers' engagement rates, including likes, comments, shares, and overall interaction levels. High engagement indicates an active and interested audience.
- **Follower Growth**: Monitor the growth of an influencer's followers over time. Steady growth suggests increasing popularity and relevance.
- **Content Quality**: Assess the quality of an influencer's content by reviewing visual aesthetics, storytelling abilities, and consistency. High-quality content is more likely to resonate with audiences.

Audience Demographics and Psychographics

- **Demographic Data**: Use analytics tools to gather demographic information about an influencer's audience, such as age, gender, location, and language. This ensures alignment with the brand's target market.
- **Psychographic Insights**: Delve into psychographic data, including audience interests, values, and lifestyle preferences. This helps in selecting influencers whose followers are more likely to connect with the brand's message.

Campaign Planning and Strategy

Data and analytics are invaluable for developing effective campaign strategies. By understanding past performance and audience behavior, brands can create more targeted and impactful campaigns.

Historical Data Analysis

- **Previous Campaign Performance**: Review the performance of past campaigns to identify what worked and what didn't. Look at metrics like reach, engagement, conversion rates, and ROI.
- **Benchmarking**: Establish benchmarks based on previous campaigns and industry standards. This provides a reference point for measuring the success of new campaigns.

Audience Segmentation

- **Segmentation Strategies**: Use data to segment the target audience into distinct groups based on demographics, behavior, and interests. Tailor content and messaging to each segment for maximum relevance and impact.
- **Personalized Campaigns**: Develop personalized campaigns that cater to the specific needs and preferences of each audience segment. Personalized content is more likely to engage and convert.

Real-Time Monitoring and Optimization

Once a campaign is live, real-time data monitoring allows for ongoing optimization to enhance performance and achieve better results.

Performance Tracking

- **Key Performance Indicators (KPIs)**: Define and monitor KPIs such as reach, engagement, click-through rates, and conversions. These metrics provide insights into the effectiveness of the campaign.
- **Real-Time Analytics Tools**: Utilize real-time analytics tools to track campaign performance as it unfolds. This enables immediate adjustments and optimizations based on current data.

A/B Testing

- **Content Variations**: Implement A/B testing to compare different versions of content, such as headlines, visuals, and calls to action. Analyze which variations perform best and use the insights to refine the campaign.
- **Data-Driven Decisions**: Make data-driven decisions to optimize campaign elements in real time. This can include adjusting targeting parameters, modifying content, and reallocating budgets to better-performing segments.

Measuring ROI and Effectiveness

Measuring the return on investment (ROI) and overall effectiveness of influencer marketing campaigns is essential for understanding their impact and justifying the investment.

Attribution Models

- **Multi-Touch Attribution**: Implement multi-touch attribution models to understand the contribution of each touchpoint in the customer journey. This provides a comprehensive view of how influencer marketing fits into the broader marketing strategy.
- **Conversion Tracking**: Use conversion tracking tools to measure the direct impact of influencer campaigns on sales, leads, and other conversion goals.

ROI Calculation

- **Cost Analysis**: Calculate the total cost of the campaign, including influencer fees, production costs, and any additional expenses. Compare this against the revenue generated or the value of achieved objectives.
- **Performance Metrics**: Analyze performance metrics to determine the overall effectiveness of the campaign. Metrics such as engagement rates, conversion rates, and customer acquisition costs provide insights into the campaign's success.

Future Trends in Data and Analytics

The future of influencer marketing will see even greater integration of advanced data and analytics tools, enabling more precise targeting, improved measurement, and enhanced campaign optimization.

AI and Machine Learning

- **Predictive Analytics**: AI and machine learning will play a significant role in predictive analytics, helping brands anticipate trends, forecast campaign outcomes, and make proactive adjustments.
- **Automated Insights**: Automation will streamline the analysis process, providing real-time insights and recommendations to optimize campaigns dynamically.

Advanced Audience Insights

- **Behavioral Analysis**: Advanced tools will offer deeper insights into audience behavior, preferences, and motivations, allowing for more refined and effective targeting.
- **Sentiment Analysis**: Sentiment analysis tools will gauge audience reactions and sentiments in real time, helping brands adjust their strategies to align with audience perceptions.

Leveraging data and analytics in influencer marketing is crucial for developing effective strategies, optimizing campaigns, and achieving measurable results. By utilizing data-driven insights, brands can select the right influencers, plan targeted campaigns, monitor performance in real time, and measure ROI accurately. As data and analytics tools continue to evolve, brands that embrace these technologies will be better positioned to succeed in the competitive landscape of influencer marketing.

7.2 Integrating Influencer Marketing with Other Channels

Integrating influencer marketing with other marketing channels creates a cohesive and comprehensive strategy that amplifies brand messaging and enhances overall campaign effectiveness. This multi-channel approach ensures that the brand's message reaches a wider audience, reinforces its impact, and drives more significant results.

Creating a Unified Brand Experience

A unified brand experience across all channels ensures consistency in messaging and branding, which strengthens brand recognition and trust.

Consistent Messaging

- **Brand Voice and Tone**: Maintain a consistent brand voice and tone across all channels, including social media, email, website, and offline marketing efforts. This helps in creating a cohesive brand identity.
- **Key Messages**: Ensure that key messages are communicated consistently across all platforms. Influencers should be briefed on

the brand's core messages to align their content with the overall campaign.

Visual Identity

- **Brand Aesthetics**: Use consistent visual elements such as logos, color schemes, and typography across all marketing materials. This creates a recognizable and professional brand image.
- **Co-branded content**: Collaborate with influencers to create co-branded content that aligns with the brand's visual identity. This can include branded hashtags, logos, and templates.

Leveraging Social Media Synergy

Social media platforms are pivotal in influencer marketing, and integrating efforts across multiple platforms can amplify reach and engagement.

Cross-Platform Campaigns

- **Platform-Specific Content**: Tailor content to leverage the unique features and strengths of each platform. For example, use Instagram for visually appealing posts, TikTok for short, engaging videos, and Twitter for real-time interactions.
- **Hashtag Campaigns**: Create unified hashtag campaigns that encourage user-generated content across various social media platforms. This increases visibility and engagement.

Collaborative Promotions

- **Influencer Takeovers**: Arrange influencer takeovers on the brand's social media accounts to provide fresh content and reach new audiences. This also adds a personal touch to the brand's online presence.
- **Live Collaborations**: Host live events, such as Q&A sessions, product launches, or tutorials, where influencers and brand representatives collaborate in real time. This interactive approach engages audiences and drives immediate feedback.

Enhancing Email Marketing

Email marketing remains a powerful channel for direct communication with customers. Integrating influencer marketing into email campaigns can boost open rates and engagement.

Influencer Endorsements

- **Testimonials and Reviews**: Include influencer testimonials and reviews in email newsletters to build credibility and trust. Highlight the influencer's experience with the product or service.
- **Exclusive Content**: Offer exclusive content or promotions from influencers to email subscribers. This can include early access to new products, special discounts, or personalized messages from influencers.

Storytelling

- **Campaign Narratives**: Incorporate influencer stories and experiences into email campaigns to create compelling narratives. This approach humanizes the brand and makes the content more relatable.
- **Behind-the-scenes**: Share behind-the-scenes content featuring influencers to provide a glimpse into the collaboration process. This builds transparency and strengthens the connection with the audience.

Boosting Content Marketing

Content marketing, including blog posts, articles, and videos, benefits significantly from the integration of influencer marketing.

Guest Blogging

- **Influencer Contributions**: Invite influencers to contribute guest blog posts or articles on the brand's website. This provides valuable content for the audience and leverages the influencer's expertise and reach.
- **Collaborative Content**: Co-create content with influencers, such as how-to guides, tutorials, or case studies. This enriches the brand's content library and offers diverse perspectives.

Video Marketing

- **Influencer Features**: Feature influencers in branded video content, such as product demonstrations, unboxings, or interviews. Video content is highly engaging and effectively communicates the brand's message.
- **Webinars and Live Streams**: Host webinars or live streams with influencers to discuss relevant topics, answer audience questions, and promote products. This interactive format encourages real-time engagement and provides valuable insights.

Integrating Offline and Online Efforts

Combining offline and online marketing efforts ensures a seamless brand experience and maximizes campaign reach.

Event Marketing

- **Influencer Appearances**: Invite influencers to participate in offline events such as product launches, trade shows, or brand activations. Their presence can attract more attendees and generate buzz.
- **Event Coverage**: Utilize influencers to cover offline events on their social media channels, providing real-time updates and engaging content. This extends the event's reach to a broader online audience.

Print and Digital Synergy

- **Print Collaborations**: Feature influencers in print advertisements, magazines, or brochures to bridge the gap between offline and online marketing. This can drive offline audiences to the brand's online platforms.
- **QR Codes and Links**: Include QR codes or direct links in print materials that lead to influencer content or brand websites. This encourages offline audiences to engage with the brand online.

Measuring Integrated Campaign Success

To assess the effectiveness of integrated influencer marketing campaigns, it is essential to track performance across all channels.

Unified Analytics

- **Comprehensive Metrics**: Use unified analytics tools to track key performance indicators (KPIs) such as reach, engagement, conversions, and ROI across all marketing channels. This provides a holistic view of the campaign's success.
- **Cross-Channel Attribution**: Implement cross-channel attribution models to understand the contribution of each channel to the overall campaign goals. This helps in identifying the most effective channels and optimizing future strategies.

Continuous Optimization

- **Data-Driven Adjustments**: Regularly analyze performance data to identify areas for improvement. Make data-driven adjustments to optimize content, targeting, and allocation of resources.
- **Feedback Loop**: Establish a feedback loop with influencers and internal teams to gather insights and refine strategies. This collaborative approach ensures continuous improvement and better alignment with campaign objectives.

Integrating influencer marketing with other channels creates a unified, cohesive strategy that enhances brand visibility and engagement. By maintaining consistent messaging, leveraging the strengths of different platforms, and combining online and offline efforts, brands can amplify the impact of their influencer campaigns. Measuring and optimizing the performance of these integrated campaigns ensures long-term success and a stronger connection with the audience.

7.3 The Rise of Virtual Influencers and AI

The landscape of influencer marketing is evolving rapidly, with the rise of virtual influencers and artificial intelligence (AI) transforming how brands connect with audiences. Virtual influencers, digital characters created through CGI and AI, offer unique opportunities and challenges. As AI technology advances, it is reshaping the strategies and capabilities within influencer marketing.

Understanding Virtual Influencers

Virtual influencers are computer-generated characters designed to appear and behave like real humans. They can be entirely fictional or modeled after real people, and they interact with audiences through social media platforms.

Creation and Characteristics

- **CGI and AI Technology**: Virtual influencers are created using advanced CGI (computer-generated imagery) and AI technology. This allows for highly realistic and customizable characters.
- **Distinct Personalities**: Each virtual influencer has a distinct personality, style, and backstory. These attributes are carefully crafted to resonate with target audiences and align with brand values.
- **Controlled Narrative**: Unlike human influencers, virtual influencers offer complete control over the narrative, ensuring consistent messaging and behavior aligned with the brand's goals.

Examples of Popular Virtual Influencers

- **Lil Miquela**: One of the most well-known virtual influencers, Lil Miquela has millions of followers on Instagram and collaborates with major brands. Her posts and persona blend seamlessly with real-world content.
- **Shudu Gram**: Touted as the world's first digital supermodel, Shudu Gram collaborates with fashion brands and appears in high-

end magazines, showcasing the potential of virtual influencers in the fashion industry.

Benefits of Virtual Influencers

Virtual influencers offer several advantages over traditional human influencers, making them an attractive option for brands looking to innovate in influencer marketing.

Consistency and Control

- **Brand Alignment**: Virtual influencers can be designed to perfectly align with the brand's identity and messaging. This ensures a consistent and controlled representation of the brand across all content.
- **Predictable Behavior**: Brands have full control over the behavior and actions of virtual influencers, eliminating risks associated with human influencers, such as scandals or off-brand behavior.

Scalability and Flexibility

- **24/7 Availability**: Virtual influencers are not bound by time zones or physical limitations. They can engage with audiences around the clock and participate in multiple campaigns simultaneously.
- **Creative Flexibility**: Brands can push creative boundaries with virtual influencers, using them in a wide range of scenarios and

settings that might be impractical or impossible for human influencers.

Cost Efficiency

- **Long-Term Investment**: While the initial creation of a virtual influencer can be costly, they offer long-term cost efficiency. Brands do not need to pay for travel, accommodation, or ongoing endorsement fees.
- **Reusability**: Virtual influencers can be reused across multiple campaigns, reducing the need for continuous recruitment and training of new influencers.

Challenges and Considerations

Despite the benefits, the use of virtual influencers comes with its own set of challenges and ethical considerations.

Authenticity and Trust

- **Perceived Authenticity**: One of the biggest challenges is convincing audiences of the authenticity of virtual influencers. Unlike human influencers, virtual characters can lack the perceived authenticity and relatability that drive trust and engagement.
- **Transparency**: Brands must be transparent about the virtual nature of these influencers to maintain credibility. Deceptive practices can lead to backlash and damage brand reputation.

Technical and Creative Demands

- **High Production Costs**: Creating and maintaining high-quality virtual influencers requires significant investment in technology and creative resources. This can be a barrier for smaller brands with limited budgets.
- **Continuous Innovation**: To keep virtual influencers engaging and relevant, brands need to continuously innovate and update their personas, content, and interactions.

Ethical Concerns

- **Representation and Diversity**: There are ethical considerations regarding the representation and diversity of virtual influencers. Brands must ensure that these digital characters promote positive and inclusive messages.
- **Impact on Human Influencers**: The rise of virtual influencers may impact the livelihoods of human influencers. Brands should consider the broader implications of their marketing strategies on the influencer ecosystem.

AI in Influencer Marketing

AI technology is revolutionizing influencer marketing by enhancing data analysis, campaign optimization, and audience targeting.

Data Analysis and Insights

- **Advanced Analytics**: AI-powered tools can analyze vast amounts of data to identify trends, measure campaign performance, and gain deeper insights into audience behavior. This enables more informed decision-making.
- **Predictive Modeling**: AI can predict the success of influencer campaigns by analyzing historical data and current trends. This helps brands optimize their strategies and allocate resources more effectively.

Campaign Optimization

- **Content Personalization**: AI enables the creation of highly personalized content tailored to specific audience segments. This increases relevance and engagement, leading to better campaign outcomes.
- **Real-Time Adjustments**: AI can monitor campaign performance in real time and suggest adjustments to optimize results. This includes modifying content, targeting, and budget allocation.

Audience Targeting

- **Precise Targeting**: AI algorithms can identify the most relevant influencers and audience segments for a campaign, ensuring that the brand's message reaches the right people.

- **Behavioral Insights**: AI provides insights into audience preferences, behaviors, and sentiment, allowing brands to craft more effective and resonant campaigns.

Future Trends and Opportunities

The rise of virtual influencers and AI opens up new possibilities and trends in influencer marketing.

Integration with Emerging Technologies

- **Augmented Reality (AR)**: Virtual influencers can be integrated with AR to create immersive and interactive experiences. For example, AR filters featuring virtual influencers can engage users in unique ways.
- **Virtual Reality (VR)**: VR offers opportunities for virtual influencers to participate in virtual events, concerts, and interactive brand experiences, providing a new level of engagement.

Enhanced Personalization

- **Hyper-Targeted Campaigns**: AI will enable even more precise targeting and personalization, creating hyper-targeted campaigns that resonate deeply with individual audience members.
- **Adaptive Content**: AI can create adaptive content that changes based on user interactions and preferences, offering a more dynamic and personalized experience.

Sustainability and Ethics

- **Sustainable Practices**: The use of virtual influencers can reduce the environmental impact of traditional influencer campaigns, such as travel and production costs. Brands can leverage this to promote sustainability.
- **Ethical Standards**: As the industry evolves, establishing ethical standards for the use of virtual influencers and AI will be crucial. This includes ensuring transparency, diversity, and positive representation.

The rise of virtual influencers and AI is transforming the influencer marketing landscape, offering new opportunities for brands to connect with audiences in innovative ways. By leveraging the benefits of virtual influencers and AI-driven insights, brands can create more engaging, personalized, and effective campaigns. However, they must also navigate the challenges and ethical considerations associated with these technologies to maintain authenticity and trust. As the industry continues to evolve, staying at the forefront of these trends will be essential for brands looking to succeed in the competitive world of influencer marketing.

7.4 Influencer Marketing in Niche Markets

Influencer marketing in niche markets presents unique opportunities and challenges. While niche markets may have smaller audiences compared to mainstream markets, they often feature highly engaged and passionate communities. Leveraging influencer marketing within these specialized segments requires a strategic approach to identify the right influencers, create tailored content, and foster authentic relationships.

Understanding Niche Markets

Niche markets cater to specific segments of the population with specialized interests, needs, and preferences. These markets can range from hobbyist communities, like gaming and knitting, to professional fields such as finance and healthcare. Understanding the nuances of these markets is crucial for effective influencer marketing.

Characteristics of Niche Markets

- **Specific Interests**: Niche markets are defined by specific interests and preferences. The content must be tailored to these unique characteristics to resonate with the audience.
- **High Engagement**: Audiences in niche markets tend to be more engaged and loyal. They value detailed, high-quality content that addresses their particular interests.
- **Expertise and Authenticity**: Influencers in niche markets are often seen as experts in their field. Authenticity and credibility are critical for success in these segments.

Identifying Influencers in Niche Markets

Finding the right influencers in niche markets requires a targeted approach. These influencers may not have massive followings, but their influence within their specific community can be significant.

Research and Discovery

- **Specialized Platforms**: Utilize platforms that cater to specific niches. For example, LinkedIn is effective for professional niches, while Reddit and niche-specific forums can help identify influencers in hobbyist communities.
- **Hashtag Analysis**: Analyze hashtags and keywords relevant to the niche market to discover active and influential users who consistently engage with niche content.
- **Community Involvement**: Participate in online communities related to the niche market. This can provide insights into key influencers and the type of content that resonates with the audience.

Evaluating Influence and Fit

- **Relevance**: Ensure that the influencer's content aligns with the niche and appeals to the target audience. Their expertise and interests should match the brand's offerings.
- **Engagement Metrics**: Focus on engagement metrics rather than follower count. High engagement rates indicate a strong connection with the audience and a greater potential for influence.
- **Content Quality**: Assess the quality and authenticity of the influencer's content. High-quality, informative, and engaging content is essential for maintaining credibility in niche markets.

Creating Tailored Content

Content tailored to niche markets should address the specific interests and needs of the audience. This requires a deep understanding of the niche and a collaborative approach with influencers.

Collaborative Content Creation

- **Co-Creation**: Work closely with influencers to co-create content that combines the brand's message with the influencer's unique perspective and expertise. This ensures authenticity and relevance.
- **Educational Content**: In many niche markets, audiences seek educational and informative content. Tutorials, how-to guides, and in-depth reviews can be particularly effective.
- **Storytelling**: Use storytelling to create compelling narratives that resonate with the niche audience. Highlighting real-life experiences and case studies can enhance credibility and engagement.

Content Formats

- **Long-Form Content**: For niches that value detailed information, long-form content such as blog posts, podcasts, and YouTube videos can be highly effective.
- **Visual Content**: In visually oriented niches, such as fashion, art, and food, high-quality images and videos are essential. Platforms like Instagram and Pinterest are ideal for these markets.

- **Interactive Content**: Engage the audience with interactive content such as live streams, Q&A sessions, and polls. This fosters community interaction and enhances engagement.

Building Authentic Relationships

Building authentic relationships with influencers is crucial in niche markets. These relationships should be based on mutual respect, trust, and shared values.

Engagement and Communication

- **Open Dialogue**: Maintain open and transparent communication with influencers. Regularly discuss campaign goals, expectations, and feedback to ensure alignment and collaboration.
- **Support and Recognition**: Show appreciation for the influencer's contributions by recognizing their efforts and providing support. This can include sharing their content, providing exclusive opportunities, and featuring them in brand communications.

Long-Term Partnerships

- **Consistency**: Establish long-term partnerships with influencers to create a consistent presence in the niche market. Consistency helps build trust and familiarity with the audience.

- **Exclusive Collaborations**: Offer exclusive collaborations and content opportunities to influencers. This not only strengthens the partnership but also provides unique value to the audience.

Measuring Success in Niche Markets

Measuring the success of influencer marketing campaigns in niche markets requires focusing on metrics that reflect engagement, relevance, and impact rather than sheer volume.

Key Performance Indicators (KPIs)

- **Engagement Rates**: Track metrics such as likes, comments, shares, and direct interactions to gauge audience engagement.
- **Traffic and Conversions**: Monitor website traffic, leads, and conversions generated from influencer content to assess the campaign's impact on business goals.
- **Brand Sentiment**: Analyze brand sentiment through comments, feedback, and social listening tools to understand the audience's perception and response to the campaign.

Qualitative Feedback

- **Community Feedback**: Gather feedback from the niche community through surveys, direct comments, and conversations. This provides valuable insights into the campaign's effectiveness and areas for improvement.

- **Influencer Insights**: Collaborate with influencers to gather their insights and observations about the campaign. Influencers often have a deep understanding of their audience and can provide valuable feedback.

Future Trends in Niche Influencer Marketing

As niche markets continue to grow and evolve, several trends are shaping the future of influencer marketing in these segments.

Micro and Nano Influencers

- **Increased Focus**: Brands are increasingly recognizing the value of micro and nano influencers who have smaller but highly engaged and loyal followings within niche markets.
- **Authentic Connections**: These influencers often have more personal and authentic connections with their audience, making them powerful advocates for niche brands.

Community-Driven Campaigns

- **Crowdsourcing Content**: Involving the niche community in content creation and campaign ideation can enhance engagement and foster a sense of ownership and loyalty.
- **User-Generated Content**: Encouraging user-generated content helps build a vibrant community around the brand and leverages the passion and creativity of the audience.

Technology and Innovation

- **AI and Data Analytics**: Advanced AI and data analytics tools can provide deeper insights into niche audiences, enabling more precise targeting and personalized content.
- **Virtual and Augmented Reality**: VR and AR technologies offer innovative ways to engage niche audiences with immersive and interactive experiences.

Influencer marketing in niche markets offers unique opportunities for brands to connect with highly engaged and passionate communities. By understanding the characteristics of niche markets, identifying the right influencers, creating tailored content, and building authentic relationships, brands can achieve significant impact and drive meaningful engagement. As the landscape continues to evolve, staying attuned to emerging trends and leveraging technology will be essential for success in niche influencer marketing.

7.5 Future Trends to Watch in 2024 and Beyond

Influencer marketing is continuously evolving, driven by technological advancements, changing consumer behaviors, and the emergence of new platforms. As we move further into 2024 and beyond, several key trends are poised to shape the future of influencer marketing. Staying ahead of these trends will be crucial for brands looking to leverage influencer marketing effectively.

Increased Use of AI and Machine Learning

Artificial Intelligence (AI) and Machine Learning (ML) are revolutionizing influencer marketing by providing advanced tools for data analysis, campaign optimization, and audience targeting.

Advanced Analytics

- **Predictive Analytics**: AI can predict campaign outcomes by analyzing historical data, helping brands to optimize strategies and improve ROI.
- **Sentiment Analysis**: AI tools can analyze social media conversations to gauge audience sentiment and identify trends, enabling brands to tailor their messaging accordingly.

Content Creation

- **AI-Generated Content**: AI can assist in creating personalized content at scale, including text, images, and videos. This allows for more efficient content production and greater customization.
- **Virtual Influencers**: The development of AI-powered virtual influencers, as discussed earlier, will continue to grow, providing brands with unique opportunities to engage audiences.

Campaign Optimization

- **Real-Time Adjustments**: AI can monitor campaign performance in real time and suggest adjustments to optimize results, such as modifying content or reallocating budgets.
- **Enhanced Targeting**: Machine learning algorithms can identify the most relevant influencers and audience segments, ensuring that campaigns reach the right people.

Rise of Short-Form Video Content

Short-form video content, popularized by platforms like TikTok and Instagram Reels, will remain a dominant trend in influencer marketing.

Platform Growth

- **TikTok and Reels**: The popularity of TikTok and Instagram Reels continues to grow, making them essential platforms for influencer marketing. Brands need to create engaging, bite-sized content to capture the audience's attention.
- **Emerging Platforms**: New platforms focused on short-form video content are likely to emerge, providing additional opportunities for brands to reach younger audiences.

Creative Storytelling

- **Engaging Content**: Short-form videos require concise and compelling storytelling. Brands and influencers will need to focus on creativity and originality to stand out.
- **Interactive Elements**: Features like polls, challenges, and interactive filters will enhance engagement and make content more interactive and shareable.

Focus on Authenticity and Transparency

As consumers become more discerning, authenticity and transparency in influencer marketing will be more important than ever.

Authentic Relationships

- **Genuine Partnerships**: Brands will prioritize long-term partnerships with influencers who genuinely align with their values and ethos, fostering deeper and more authentic connections.
- **Influencer Authenticity**: Audiences value influencers who are genuine and transparent about their experiences. Authenticity will be key to maintaining trust and engagement.

Transparency in Marketing

- **Clear Disclosure**: Compliance with regulations such as the FTC guidelines on sponsored content will remain critical. Clear and honest disclosure of sponsored content will build trust with audiences.
- **Ethical Marketing**: Brands will need to ensure their influencer marketing practices are ethical, avoiding misleading claims and promoting positive and inclusive messages.

Niche and Micro-Influencers

The trend towards using niche and micro-influencers will continue to grow, driven by their highly engaged audiences and authentic connections.

Targeted Engagement

- **Community Focus**: Micro-influencers often have deep connections within specific communities. Brands can leverage these influencers to reach niche audiences with highly targeted content.
- **Higher Engagement Rates**: Micro-influencers typically have higher engagement rates compared to macro-influencers, making their campaigns more effective in driving interaction and conversion.

Cost-Effectiveness

- **Budget-Friendly**: Collaborating with micro-influencers can be more cost-effective than working with high-profile influencers, providing a better return on investment for brands with limited budgets.
- **Scalability**: Brands can collaborate with multiple micro-influencers to scale their campaigns and reach a broader audience without compromising authenticity.

Integration of Social Commerce

Social commerce, the convergence of social media and e-commerce, is transforming how consumers shop online. Influencer marketing will play a pivotal role in driving social commerce.

Shoppable Content

- **In-App Purchases**: Platforms like Instagram and TikTok are enhancing their shopping features, allowing users to make purchases directly within the app. Influencers can create shoppable content that drives instant sales.
- **Product Tagging**: Influencers can tag products in their posts and stories, providing a seamless shopping experience for their followers.

Live Shopping

- **Live Stream Shopping**: Influencers hosting live shopping events will become more common, allowing them to showcase products, answer questions in real time, and drive immediate purchases.
- **Interactive Experiences**: Live shopping combines entertainment and shopping, creating engaging and interactive experiences that boost consumer interest and sales.

Emphasis on Data Privacy and Security

With increasing concerns about data privacy and security, brands will need to prioritize transparent and ethical data practices.

Compliance with Regulations

- **Data Protection Laws**: Compliance with data protection laws such as GDPR and CCPA will be essential. Brands must ensure they handle consumer data responsibly and transparently.
- **Consumer Trust**: Transparent data practices and a commitment to protecting consumer privacy will build trust and loyalty among audiences.

Secure Influencer Collaborations

- **Data Security**: Ensuring the security of data shared between brands and influencers will be crucial. This includes secure communication channels and data handling practices.
- **Ethical Data Use**: Brands must use data ethically, avoiding invasive tracking practices and respecting consumer privacy preferences.

Sustainability and Social Responsibility

Consumers increasingly expect brands to demonstrate social responsibility and sustainability in their marketing efforts.

Sustainable Practices

- **Eco-Friendly Campaigns**: Brands will focus on creating eco-friendly influencer marketing campaigns that promote sustainability and environmental consciousness.
- **Responsible Collaborations**: Partnering with influencers who advocate for social and environmental causes will enhance brand credibility and appeal to socially conscious consumers.

Corporate Social Responsibility (CSR)

- **Cause Marketing**: Collaborating with influencers on because marketing campaigns will highlight the brand's commitment to social responsibility and drive positive social impact.

- **Transparency and Accountability**: Brands must be transparent about their CSR initiatives and demonstrate tangible actions and results.

The future of influencer marketing is dynamic and evolving, with AI and machine learning, short-form video content, authenticity, niche influencers, social commerce, data privacy, and sustainability all playing pivotal roles. Brands that stay ahead of these trends and adapt their strategies accordingly will be well-positioned to connect with audiences, drive engagement, and achieve their marketing goals in 2024 and beyond. Embracing innovation while maintaining ethical and transparent practices will be key to building lasting relationships with consumers and achieving long-term success in the ever-changing landscape of influencer marketing.

Chapter 8: Measuring ROI and Long-Term Impact

Influencer marketing, like any other marketing strategy, requires thorough evaluation to assess its effectiveness and long-term impact on business objectives. Measuring return on investment (ROI) and understanding the broader impact of influencer campaigns are crucial for optimizing future strategies and demonstrating value to stakeholders.

1. Understanding ROI in Influencer Marketing

Measuring ROI in influencer marketing involves quantifying the financial outcomes generated relative to the investment made in the campaign. It goes beyond simple metrics like engagement rates and follower growth to assess tangible business outcomes.

Key Elements of ROI Measurement:

- **Cost Analysis**: Calculate the total investment in the influencer campaign, including fees paid to influencers, production costs, and any associated expenses (e.g., travel, giveaways).
- **Revenue Generation**: Track direct revenue generated from the campaign, such as sales attributed to influencer promotions using unique discount codes or affiliate links.
- **Attribution Modeling**: Use attribution models to determine how influencer activities contributed to conversions and sales. This may involve multi-touch attribution models that credit influencers for various stages of the customer journey.

- **Lifetime Value (LTV)**: Evaluate the long-term impact of influencer campaigns by assessing customer LTV. Consider how influencer-driven acquisitions contribute to recurring revenue and customer retention.

2. Metrics for Measuring Influencer Marketing ROI

Selecting appropriate metrics is crucial for accurately measuring influencer marketing ROI. These metrics should align with campaign objectives and provide actionable insights into performance.

Key Metrics to Consider:

- **Conversion Rate**: Measure the percentage of website visitors who complete a desired action, such as making a purchase or signing up for a newsletter, after engaging with influencer content.
- **Return on Ad Spend (ROAS)**: Calculate the revenue generated from influencer campaigns divided by the total campaign spend. This metric quantifies the efficiency of marketing investments.
- **Engagement Metrics**: Track likes, comments, shares, and other interactions to gauge audience engagement with influencer content. Higher engagement rates indicate content resonance and audience interest.
- **Reach and Impressions**: Evaluate the reach of influencer content to assess brand visibility and exposure. Impressions indicate the number of times content was displayed, providing insights into potential audience size.

3. Long-Term Impact of Influencer Marketing

Assessing the long-term impact of influencer marketing extends beyond immediate campaign outcomes to evaluate lasting benefits and brand equity.

Considerations for Long-Term Impact:

- **Brand Awareness**: Measure changes in brand awareness and perception following influencer collaborations. Surveys, brand sentiment analysis, and social listening tools can provide qualitative insights.
- **Audience Growth**: Analyze follower growth and audience demographics over time to understand how influencer partnerships contribute to audience expansion and market reach.
- **Content Evergreenness**: Evaluate the longevity and ongoing value of influencer-generated content. Evergreen content continues to drive engagement and SEO benefits long after the campaign ends.
- **Partnership Continuity**: Assess the impact of sustained influencer partnerships on brand loyalty and customer retention. Repeat collaborations can strengthen relationships and maintain brand presence.

4. Tools and Techniques for ROI Measurement

Utilize advanced tools and techniques to streamline ROI measurement and gain deeper insights into influencer campaign performance.

- **Analytics Platforms**: Leverage analytics platforms like Google Analytics, social media insights, and influencer marketing software to track performance metrics and campaign attribution.
- **Attribution Models**: Implement attribution models (e.g., first-touch, last-touch, linear attribution) to accurately attribute conversions to influencer interactions across multiple touchpoints.
- **Data Integration**: Integrate influencer campaign data with CRM systems and marketing automation platforms to unify data sources and track influencer-driven conversions.
- **Survey and Feedback**: Collect audience feedback through surveys and polls to gauge the impact of influencer content on brand perception and purchase decisions.

Measuring ROI and long-term impact in influencer marketing requires a strategic approach, combining quantitative metrics with qualitative insights. By evaluating financial outcomes, audience engagement, and broader brand effects, marketers can optimize campaigns, demonstrate value, and align influencer strategies with overall business objectives effectively. Continuous refinement of measurement techniques and adaptation to industry trends will be essential for maximizing the effectiveness of influencer marketing investments in the evolving digital landscape.

8.1 Calculating ROI in Influencer Marketing

Calculating ROI in influencer marketing involves assessing the financial return generated from your investment in influencer campaigns. Here's how you can approach it:

Understanding ROI in Influencer Marketing

ROI (Return on Investment) in influencer marketing measures the profitability of your campaigns relative to the costs incurred. It helps determine whether your investment in influencer partnerships is yielding positive financial outcomes.

Key Components of ROI Calculation:

Costs of the Campaign:

- **Influencer Fees**: Total fees paid to influencers for their participation in the campaign.
- **Production Costs**: Expenses related to content creation, such as photography, videography, editing, and graphic design.
- **Promotional Costs**: Additional expenses for giveaways, sponsored posts, or ad placements associated with the campaign.

Revenue Generation:

- **Direct Sales**: Calculate revenue directly attributed to the influencer campaign. This can be tracked through unique discount codes, affiliate links, or dedicated landing pages.
- **Indirect Sales**: Estimate additional revenue influenced by the campaign, considering customer acquisitions and repeat purchases.

Attribution Modeling:

Use attribution models to attribute conversions and sales to specific influencer activities. This may involve:

- **First-Touch Attribution**: Crediting the influencer for introducing customers to the brand.
- **Last-Touch Attribution**: Giving credit to the influencer for the final interaction that led to a purchase.
- **Multi-Touch Attribution**: Recognizing the influencer's contribution across multiple touchpoints in the customer journey.

Calculation Formula:

To calculate ROI in influencer marketing, use the following formula:

$$ROI = \frac{(Revenue - Cost)}{Cost} \times 100$$

Where:

- **Revenue**: Total revenue generated from the influencer campaign.
- **Cost**: Total cost incurred for the influencer campaign (influencer fees + production costs + promotional costs).

Example Calculation:

Let's say you invested $5,000 in an influencer campaign, including $3,000 in influencer fees and $2,000 in production and promotional costs. The campaign generated $20,000 in revenue directly attributed to influencer-driven sales.

$$ROI = \frac{20{,}000 - 5{,}000}{5{,}000} \times 100$$

$$ROI = \frac{15{,}000}{5{,}000} \times 100$$

$$ROI = 300\%$$

Interpretation:

An ROI of 300% indicates that for every dollar invested in the influencer campaign, you generated $3 in revenue. Positive ROI signifies that the campaign was profitable.

Considerations:

- **Time Frame**: Determine the time frame for ROI calculation (e.g., monthly, quarterly, annually) based on your campaign objectives and sales cycle.
- **Cost Breakdown**: Ensure all campaign costs are accurately accounted for to calculate a comprehensive ROI.
- **Attribution Challenges**: Address challenges in attributing sales to influencer efforts, considering the influence of other marketing channels and organic growth.

By consistently measuring ROI and refining your influencer marketing strategies based on these insights, you can optimize campaign performance, allocate resources effectively, and maximize the impact of influencer partnerships on your business objectives.

8.2 Long-Term Brand Building with Influencers

Long-term brand building with influencers goes beyond immediate campaign metrics to focus on creating enduring relationships and sustainable brand growth. Here's how influencers can contribute to long-term brand building:

Establishing Brand Authority and Trust

- **Content Credibility**: Influencers help build brand authority by creating authentic, trustworthy content that resonates with their followers. Consistent messaging and genuine endorsements can strengthen brand credibility over time.
- **Audience Alignment**: Partnering with influencers whose values align with your brand fosters genuine connections with their audiences. This alignment builds trust and loyalty among consumers who value the influencer's opinions.

Cultivating Community and Engagement

- **Community Engagement**: Influencers engage directly with their followers, fostering a sense of community around your brand. This

ongoing interaction builds a loyal customer base that feels connected to both the influencer and your products.
- **Feedback Loop**: Influencers provide valuable insights through audience feedback and sentiment analysis. This information helps brands understand consumer preferences, refine product offerings, and tailor marketing strategies effectively.

Driving Long-Term Growth and Sales

- **Customer Lifetime Value**: Influencers can drive customer acquisition and retention, contributing to long-term revenue growth. Their advocacy and ongoing promotion can influence repeat purchases and customer lifetime value.
- **Sustainable Partnerships**: Establishing long-term partnerships with influencers cultivates stability and consistency in brand messaging. Regular collaborations reinforce brand values and maintain visibility in the marketplace.

Enhancing Brand Perception and Recognition

- **Brand Affinity**: Collaborating with influencers who embody your brand values enhances brand affinity among their followers. Positive associations and endorsements contribute to favorable brand perception and recognition.
- **Visibility across Platforms**: Leveraging influencers across multiple platforms increases brand visibility and reach. Consistent exposure across different audiences reinforces brand identity and facilitates market expansion.

Measuring Long-Term Impact

- **Brand Sentiment Analysis**: Monitor social media sentiment and brand mentions to gauge public perception over time. Positive sentiment and increased mentions indicate successful brand-building efforts with influencers.
- **Metrics beyond Sales**: Look beyond immediate sales metrics to measure influencer impact on brand awareness, sentiment, and customer engagement. Track metrics such as brand mentions, social shares, and engagement rates to assess long-term brand health.

8.3 Adjusting Strategies Based on Performance Data

Long-term brand building with influencers requires strategic planning, consistent engagement, and a commitment to fostering authentic relationships. By aligning with influencers who share your brand values and investing in sustainable partnerships, you can effectively leverage their influence to build brand authority, cultivate community, drive growth, and enhance brand perception over time. Continuously evaluate performance metrics and adapt strategies to maximize the long-term impact of influencer collaborations on your brand's success.

Adjusting influencer marketing strategies based on performance data is crucial for optimizing campaign effectiveness and achieving desired outcomes. Here's how you can effectively adjust your strategies:

Analyzing Performance Data

1. Key Performance Indicators (KPIs):

- **Engagement Rates**: Measure likes, comments, shares, and other interactions to assess content resonance and audience engagement.
- **Conversion Rates**: Track the percentage of users who take desired actions (e.g., purchases, sign-ups) after engaging with influencer content.
- **ROI**: Calculate the return on investment to determine the financial impact of influencer campaigns.

2. Audience Insights:

- **Demographics**: Analyze audience demographics (age, gender, location) to understand who engages most with influencer content.
- **Behavioral Data**: Use analytics tools to identify audience behaviors and preferences, informing content customization and targeting strategies.

Strategies for Adjustment

1. Content Optimization:

- **Content Analysis**: Review performance metrics to identify top-performing content types and themes. Replicate successful content strategies in future campaigns.

- **Creative Refresh**: Experiment with new content formats, visuals, or storytelling techniques based on audience preferences and engagement trends.

2. **Influencer Selection:**

- **Performance Evaluation**: Assess individual influencer performance against KPIs. Prioritize collaborations with influencers who consistently drive engagement and conversions.
- **Diversification**: Expand partnerships to include influencers with diverse audiences and niche expertise, reaching new customer segments effectively.

3. **Campaign Refinement:**

- **Messaging Adjustments**: Tailor brand messaging based on audience feedback and sentiment analysis. Align content with current trends and consumer preferences.
- **Promotional Tactics**: Test different promotional strategies (e.g., exclusive offers, and contests) to optimize campaign performance and stimulate audience interaction.

Data-Driven Decision Making

1. **Real-Time Monitoring:**

- **Performance Tracking**: Monitor campaign performance in real-time to identify early signs of success or areas needing improvement. Promptly adjust strategies to capitalize on opportunities or mitigate challenges.

2. **A/B Testing:**

- **Experimentation**: Conduct A/B tests to compare different campaign variables (e.g., content formats, posting times) and determine optimal combinations for achieving objectives.

Continuous Optimization

1. **Iterative Approach:**

- **Iterative Improvement**: Implement iterative improvements based on ongoing performance analysis. Continuously refine strategies to adapt to changing market dynamics and consumer behaviors.

2. **Feedback Loop:**

- **Stakeholder Collaboration**: Foster collaboration between marketing teams, influencers, and analytics experts. Share insights and feedback to collectively optimize influencer marketing efforts.

Adjusting influencer marketing strategies based on performance data is essential for maximizing ROI, enhancing audience engagement, and achieving long-term success. By leveraging performance insights to refine content, optimize influencer partnerships, and adapt promotional tactics, brands can effectively navigate the evolving landscape of influencer marketing and drive sustainable growth. Embrace a data-driven approach to decision-making, prioritize continuous optimization, and remain agile in responding to market feedback to maintain competitive advantage and maximize campaign impact.

8.4 Building Sustainable Influencer Partnerships

Building sustainable influencer partnerships is essential for fostering long-term relationships that benefit both brands and influencers. Here are key strategies to establish and maintain sustainable influencer partnerships:

Establishing Sustainable Influencer Partnerships

1. **Shared Values and Alignment:**

- **Brand Fit**: Select influencers whose values and audience demographics align with your brand. This alignment ensures authenticity and resonates with the influencer's followers.
- **Long-Term Vision**: Communicate your brand's long-term goals and vision to influencers. Seek partners who are committed to supporting your brand journey and evolving alongside it.

2. Clear Communication and Expectations:

- **Transparent Collaboration**: Establish clear expectations regarding campaign objectives, deliverables, timelines, and compensation. Maintain open communication to build trust and alignment throughout the partnership.
- **Feedback Mechanism**: Create a feedback loop where both parties can provide constructive feedback to improve collaboration and optimize campaign outcomes.

Nurturing Long-Term Relationships

1. Mutual Value Exchange:

- **Value Proposition**: Offer influencers value beyond monetary compensation, such as exclusive access, product insights, or co-creation opportunities. Show appreciation for their expertise and contribution to your brand's success.
- **Co-Creation**: Involve influencers in campaign ideation and content creation processes. Empower them to showcase their creativity and authenticity while aligning with brand guidelines.

2. Consistent Engagement and Support:

- **Personalized Approach**: Build personalized relationships with influencers based on their preferences and communication styles.

Stay engaged with regular updates, industry insights, and collaborative opportunities.
- **Supportive Environment**: Provide influencers with the resources, tools, and support needed to execute campaigns effectively. Address their concerns promptly and prioritize their success as brand advocates.

Measuring Partnership Success

1. **Performance Metrics and Evaluation:**

- **Performance Tracking**: Use relevant KPIs (e.g., engagement rates, conversion metrics, ROI) to evaluate the impact of influencer collaborations. Measure both quantitative and qualitative outcomes to gauge partnership effectiveness.
- **Long-Term Impact**: Assess the broader influence of influencer partnerships on brand perception, customer loyalty, and market share. Monitor trends in audience sentiment and brand mentions over time.

Adapting to Market Dynamics

1. **Flexibility and Adaptability:**

- **Market Insights**: Stay informed about market trends, consumer behaviors, and competitive landscape. Adapt influencer strategies accordingly to remain relevant and responsive to market changes.

- **Agility in Campaigns**: Embrace flexibility in campaign strategies and adjust tactics based on real-time performance data and feedback from influencers and consumers.

Building sustainable influencer partnerships requires a strategic approach centered on shared values, clear communication, mutual value exchange, and consistent support. By nurturing long-term relationships with influencers who align with your brand's ethos and objectives, brands can drive authentic engagement, enhance brand credibility, and achieve sustained growth in influencer marketing initiatives. Continuously evaluate partnership performance, adapt strategies to evolving market dynamics, and prioritize transparency and collaboration to foster enduring influencer relationships that deliver meaningful impact for both parties involved.

Conclusion

Influencer marketing has evolved into a cornerstone strategy for brands navigating the dynamic landscape of digital marketing in 2024. This comprehensive guide has explored the multifaceted realm of influencer partnerships, offering strategies, practical tips, and illuminating case studies to empower brands in harnessing the power of social media influencers to propel their growth.

Throughout this journey, we've delved into the fundamental principles of influencer selection, campaign planning, and performance measurement. We've witnessed how aligning brand values with influencer authenticity can foster genuine connections with audiences, driving engagement and loyalty. From mega influencers to niche market specialists, each partnership exemplifies the diversity and strategic application of influencer marketing across industries.

Strategic insights have illuminated the importance of clear objectives, transparent communication, and continuous adaptation to consumer insights. Brands have learned to navigate regulatory landscapes, ensuring ethical practices and transparency in influencer collaborations. Moreover, the integration of data analytics and ROI measurement has empowered brands to refine strategies iteratively, optimizing outcomes and demonstrating tangible business impact.

As we look ahead to the future of influencer marketing, the landscape continues to evolve with technological advancements and shifting consumer behaviors. Brands must remain agile, embracing innovation and adapting strategies to resonate authentically with their target audiences. The rise of virtual influencers, AI-driven insights, and immersive experiences presents new avenues for engagement and creativity, challenging brands to innovate while maintaining authenticity and relevance.

In conclusion, "Influencer Marketing 2024" serves as a foundational resource for marketers, entrepreneurs, and influencers alike. It underscores the transformative potential of strategic influencer partnerships in building brands, fostering community, and driving sustainable growth in the digital age. By leveraging the insights and strategies outlined in this guide, brands can navigate complexities, seize opportunities, and embark on a path toward enduring success in influencer marketing.

Harness the power of influence, cultivate meaningful connections, and embark on a journey of growth and innovation with influencer marketing—where authenticity meets opportunity in shaping the future of brand engagement.

www.ingramcontent.com/pod-product-compliance
Lightning Source LLC
Chambersburg PA
CBHW082233220526
45479CB00005B/1220